LUKE J. WILSON

The Greatest Commandment

Heart, Soul, Mind, Strength

Cover design based on a Canva template by Raytas.co

Back page photo by Isabella Fischer on Unsplash

First edition

This book was professionally typeset on Reedsy.
Find out more at reedsy.com

Dedicated to everyone who loves the pursuit of knowledge about our Lord and Saviour, Christ Jesus.

"Teacher, which commandment in the law is the greatest?" He said to him, " 'You shall love the Lord your God with all your heart and with all your soul and with all your mind.' This is the greatest and first commandment. And a second is like it: 'You shall love your neighbour as yourself.' On these two commandments hang all the Law and the Prophets."

Matthew 22:36-40

Contents

Preface

The Greatest Commandment. It's not called the "greatest" for no reason, and it's not just out of piety we refer to it that way.

No, Jesus himself called it that.

So often I think we only remember part of the commandment: and that's to love God. Maybe also to love our neighbour. But mostly God.

But often times the other aspects can be neglected: your *heart*, your *soul*, your *mind*, and your *strength*. This isn't meant to be judgement or a put-down though, but rather an encouragement to really dive into those areas again—to rediscover how to love God with all of our heart, soul, mind, and strength.

That's how we love God. And not in a haphazard way, but with *all* of those things, to their fullness as much as is humanly possible.

So with that said, I hope and pray that this small book can serve as a reminder, a reference, a resource, and an encouragement for you to scour the Scriptures that talk about these areas of our lives and then learn how to apply them in our day-to-day walk with God and our neighbours.

I

The Method

This section will lead you through a traditional monastic practice involving scriptural reading, meditation, and prayer. This practice aims to foster communion with God and deepen your understanding of His word. Instead of approaching Scripture as mere texts for study, we engage with it as the living word to be experienced and internalised, and break away from reading the Bible for knowledge or academic pursuits.

1

The Divine Reading

Be still and know that I am God.
Psalm 46:10

This is a devotional book, but not like you're probably used to. There will be very little commentary or personal thoughts around a passage of Scripture, or daily readings to take you through the year, as is common in other modern devotional books.

This book aims to take you back to a very ancient spiritual practice of the Church to aid you in your devotion and prayer to God by means of *Lectio Divina* — divine reading. Traditionally, *Lectio Divina* has four separate steps: read (*lectio*); meditate/-think (*Meditatio*); pray (*oratio*); and contemplate (*contemplatio*). The idea is to read a verse or two and let the Holy Spirit guide you through prayer and contemplation about what it means to you. This is why I've chosen not to provide commentary on the Scripture verses, allowing each reader to reflect on them personally and let the Spirit guide their understanding.

The method finds it origins in the third century in a letter by Origin to his then pupil Gregory Thaumaturgus ("wonder worker") who later became bishop of Caesarea.

In his Letter to Gregory Origen explains:

> Study first of all the **lectio** of the divine Scriptures. Study them, I say. For we need to study the divine writings deeply ... and while you study these divine works with a believing and God-pleasing intention, knock at that which is closed in them and it shall be opened to you by the porter, of whom Jesus says, "To him the gatekeeper opens".
>
> While you attend to this **lectio divina**, seek aright and with unwavering faith in God the hidden sense which is present in most passages of the divine Scriptures. And do not be content with knocking and seeking, for what is absolutely necessary for understanding divine things is **oratio**, and in urging us to this the Saviour says not only "knock and it will be opened to you", and "seek and you will find", but also "ask and it will be given you". — Epistle to Gregory, 4

Ambrose of Milan, who became bishop of Milan in 374, later learned from Origen's works on ways to interpret the Scriptures. He then introduced these methods into the Western Church and went on to hand them to Augustine, which then influenced the monastic tradition that followed.

In the sixth century, Benedict of Nursia, who is sometimes regarded as the the 'father of Western monasticism', formalised this practice within his monastic rule as what might be called "the four R's": **Read**, **Reflect**, **Respond** (in prayer), and **Rest** (in silence). This in turn was standardised by a 12th century Latin monk called Guigo II into the more familiar four steps of *lectio*, *meditatio*, *oratio*, and *contemplatio,* and then later it was reinvigorated in the 20th century in Vatican II and recommended for Roman Catholics to practice.

All of this is to say that there is a long history attached to this meditative practice of Scripture reading and prayer which stands apart from some of our modern-day methods. Over the next few pages I will go over the four steps and offer some other options you can incorporate into it as spiritual aids to help with your focus, too. Once you are comfortable with this method, you can jump into any of the following chapters and let the Holy Spirit guide you on which verses to read and contemplate on.

* * *

Let all my world be silent in your presence, Lord, so that I may hear what the Lord God may say in my heart. Your words are so softly spoken that no one can hear them except in a deep silence. But to hear them lifts him who sits alone and in silence completely above his natural powers, because he who humbles himself will be lift up. He who sits alone and listens will be raised above himself.
— Guigo II

2

Lectio

Your word is a lamp to my feet, and a light for my path.
Psalm 119:105

Read: What Does the Text Say?

Lectio is the initial stage where we engage with the text in a straightforward and attentive manner. The purpose is to understand the literal meaning of the text, to grasp what the words are explicitly saying. This step is about encountering the text as it is, without interpretation or personal reflection— those come later.

Preparation for Lectio

1. **Find a Quiet Space**: Choose a location where you can read without distractions. This space should foster an atmosphere of tranquillity and focus.

2. **Settle Your Mind**: Before you begin reading, take a few moments to calm your mind. You might start with a brief prayer, asking for openness and clarity as you read.

3. **Choose the Passage**: Select a passage of scripture from one of the sections in this book.

The Process of Lectio

1. **Read Slowly and Attentively**: Begin by reading the passage slowly. Avoid rushing. This isn't about covering a large amount of text or doing so much in a certain space of time, but about allowing the words to settle in your mind.

2. **Read Aloud**: If possible, read the passage aloud. This engages more senses and helps you hear the words in a new way, providing a different perspective and enhancing your understanding.

3. **Repetition**: Read the passage multiple times. With each reading, different words or phrases may stand out. Pay attention to these elements, as they might hold particular significance, as the Holy Spirit guides you.

4. **Focus on the Literal Meaning**: At this stage, concentrate on what the text is *literally* saying. Who are the characters? What is happening? What are the key actions, words, and events? Avoid jumping to interpretation or personal application; simply understand the narrative or teaching.

Tools for Deeper Understanding

1. **Contextual Reading**: Understand the broader context of the passage. What comes before and after? How does this passage fit within the chapter, book, and the Bible as a whole? This book will generally only give you a single verse or two to focus on, but you can use that to springboard into a wider reading by using your own Bible alongside it.

2. **Consult Footnotes and Cross-References**: Many Bibles contain footnotes, cross-references, and explanatory notes. These can provide insights into the text's historical and cultural background, enhancing your understanding of the literal meaning. Go further by employing the use of a study Bible, commentary, or concordance.

3. **Use Different Translations**: Comparing different translations can illuminate subtle nuances and variations in wording that might affect your understanding. Consider versions such as the New Revised Standard Version (NRSV), Christian Standard Bible (CSB), English Standard Version (ESV), and the King James Version (KJV) (or whichever is your preferred version).

4. **Note-Taking**: Write down observations, key words, phrases, and questions that arise as you read. This practice helps to internalise the text and prepares you for deeper reflection in subsequent steps of Lectio Divina.

Reflecting on the Literal Meaning

After reading the passage multiple times and considering the context, take a moment to summarise what you have read. Answer questions like:
- What is the main message of this passage?
- Who are the primary figures, and what are they doing?
- What actions or events are described?
- What instructions or teachings are given?

Practical Example

Let's walk through an example using a well-known passage: **Matthew 22:36-40** (The Greatest Commandment).

1. **First Reading**: Read Matthew 22:36-40 slowly and attentively.
   "Teacher, which is the greatest commandment in the Law?" Jesus replied: "'Love the Lord your God with all your heart and with all your soul and with all your mind.' This is the first and greatest commandment. And the second is like it: 'Love your neighbour as yourself.' All the Law and the Prophets hang on these two commandments."

2. **Second Reading**: Read the passage again, perhaps aloud, emphasising different parts each time.

3. **Literal Observations**:

   · A question is posed to Jesus by an unnamed individual,

asking which commandment in the Law is the greatest.
- Jesus responds with two commandments:
- The first and greatest commandment: "Love the Lord your God with all your heart, soul, and mind."
- The second commandment, which is like the first: "Love your neighbour as yourself."
- Jesus concludes by stating that all the Law and the Prophets depend on these two commandments.

Concluding Lectio

After you have thoroughly read and understood the passage, take a moment to rest in this understanding. Thank God for the clarity and insights you have received. Prepare to carry this literal understanding into the next phase of Lectio Divina: *Meditatio* (Meditate), where you will begin to reflect more deeply on the text and its significance in your life.

3

Meditatio

Finally, brothers, whatever things are true, whatever things are honourable, whatever things are just, whatever things are pure, whatever things are lovely, whatever things are of good report: if there is any virtue and if there is any praise, think about these things.
Philippians 4:8

Meditate: What Does This Say to Me?

Meditatio is the second step of Lectio Divina, a practice that moves us from reading the scripture to reflecting deeply on its meaning and significance for our lives. While *Lectio* (Read) focuses on understanding what the text says, *Meditatio* (Meditate) asks us to consider what the text says to us personally. This step involves thoughtful, prayerful reflection, allowing the scripture to speak to our hearts and minds.

Preparing for Meditatio

1. **Quiet the Mind**: After completing the Lectio step, take a few moments to settle your mind and heart. Engage in a brief prayer asking for the Holy Spirit's guidance in understanding the personal message of the text.

2. **Review Your Notes**: Look back at the observations you made during Lectio. Re-read any key words or phrases that stood out to you. These elements will often be the starting points for your meditation.

3. **Create a Reflective Atmosphere**: Ensure that your environment remains conducive to deep thought. Soft lighting, a comfortable seat, and perhaps some gentle instrumental background music can help create a space where you can meditate without distraction.

The Process of Meditatio

1. **Reflect on the Passage**: Begin by re-reading the passage with an open heart, asking yourself how it speaks to your current life situation. Consider what emotions or thoughts arise as you read.

2. **Ask Reflective Questions**: Engage with the text through a series of reflective questions:
   • What words or phrases resonate with me personally?
   • How does this passage challenge or comfort me?
   • Is there a particular aspect of my life that this scripture is addressing?

· What is God trying to communicate to me through this text?

3. **Personalise the Text**: Imagine the text is written directly to you. Replace general terms with your name or personal pronouns to make the message more intimate and direct.

4. **Listen to Your Heart**: Pay attention to any feelings or intuitions that arise during your meditation. These internal movements can be indicators of the areas where God is speaking to you.

Tools for Deeper Meditation

· **Journaling**: Write down your reflections, emotions, and thoughts as you meditate. Journaling helps in processing your thoughts more deeply and can be a valuable record for future reflection.
· **Visualisation**: Close your eyes and picture the scene described in the passage. Imagine yourself as a participant or an observer within the narrative. This can bring new insights and personal connections to the scripture.
· **Dialogue with God**: Engage in a conversational prayer with God about the passage. Speak honestly about how the scripture is affecting you and listen for God's response.
· **Use of Devotional Aids**: Utilise commentaries, devotional books, or study Bibles to gain different perspectives and insights into the passage.

Practical Example

Let's continue with the passage from **Matthew 22:36-40**.

1. **First Meditation**: Re-read Matthew 22:36-40 slowly.
   "Teacher, which is the greatest commandment in the Law?"
   Jesus replied: "'Love the Lord your God with all your heart
   and with all your soul and with all your mind.' This is the first
   and greatest commandment. And the second is like it: 'Love
   your neighbour as yourself.' All the Law and the Prophets
   hang on these two commandments."

2. **Reflective Questions**:
   • **Resonance**: The phrases "with all your heart," "with all
   your soul," and "with all your mind" stand out. Reflect
   on your own dedication to loving God. Is it wholehearted?
   • **Challenge**: The commandment to "love your neighbour
   as yourself" can be challenging. Are there people in your
   life you find difficult to love? Why?
   • **Application**: How can you better love God and your
   neighbour in your daily life? Are there specific actions you
   can take?

3. **Personalisation**:
   • Replace "your" with "my" to make it personal: "Love
   the Lord *my* God with all *my* heart and with all *my* soul and
   with all *my* mind."
   • Reflect on specific neighbours (friends, family,
   colleagues) whom you are called to love as yourself.

4. **Listening to Your Heart**:

• Pay attention to any feelings of resistance, guilt, or inspiration. These feelings can guide you in understanding how the passage is speaking to you.

• Notice if there is a sense of peace or discomfort. This can indicate areas of your life that may need attention or change.

Concluding Meditatio

After spending time in meditation, take a moment to summarise your insights. Write them down or share them in prayer, thanking God for the guidance and wisdom you have received. This prepares you for the next step in Lectio Divina: *Oratio* (Pray), where you will respond to God in prayer based on your reflections.

4

Oratio

Continue steadfastly in prayer, watching in it with thanksgiving
Colossians 4:2

Pray: What Can I Say to the Lord About It?

Oratio is the third step in the Lectio Divina practice, following *Lectio* (Read) and *Meditatio* (Meditate). After immersing ourselves in the text and reflecting on its personal significance, we now turn to prayer. *Oratio* invites us to enter into a dialogue with God, responding to what we have read and meditated upon. This step is about expressing our thoughts, emotions, and desires to the Lord, deepening our relationship with Him through honest and heartfelt communication.

Preparing for Oratio

1. **Create a Prayerful Environment**: Ensure your surroundings support a prayerful attitude. Find a quiet, comfortable space where you can speak with God without interruptions.
2. **Set Your Intention**: Take a moment to focus your mind and heart on the intention of praying. A short prayer asking for the Holy Spirit's presence and guidance can help centre your thoughts. Historically, the "Jesus Prayer" has also been used to focus and centre your mind on God: *Lord Jesus Christ, Son of God, have mercy on me a sinner.*
3. **Review Your Reflections**: Look back at the insights and emotions you recorded during *Meditatio*. These reflections will form the basis of your prayers.

The Process of Oratio

1. **Speak Honestly to God**: Begin by expressing your honest thoughts and feelings to God about the scripture passage. Share your struggles, joys, and any inspiration and revelations you have experienced.
2. **Praise and Thank God**: Acknowledge God's presence and goodness. Thank Him for the insights gained during your reading and meditation. Praise Him for His wisdom, love, and guidance.
3. **Confession and Petition**: Confess any shortcomings or areas where you feel challenged by the text. Ask for God's help and strength to overcome these challenges. Present your needs and requests to God, seeking His assistance and intervention.
4. **Listen for God's Response**: After speaking, take time

17

to listen. Prayer is a two-way conversation, and it's important to remain open to God's voice. Be attentive to any thoughts, feelings, or impressions that arise during this quiet time.

Tools for Deeper Prayer

1. **Prayer Journaling**: Write down your prayers, capturing your thoughts and emotions as you speak with God. This practice helps you to clarify your prayers and provides a record of your spiritual journey.
2. **Pray with Scripture**: Use the passage you have meditated on as a basis for your prayers. Incorporate specific verses into your dialogue with God, making your prayer grounded in the Scriptures.
3. **Use Prayer Prompts**: If you find it difficult to start, use prompts such as:
   "Lord, I thank You for..."
   "God, help me to..."
   "Father, I confess that..."
   "Jesus, I am grateful for..."
4. **Incorporate Silence**: Allow moments of silence within your prayer time. This quietness provides space for God to speak and for you to listen more deeply.

Practical Example

Let's continue with the passage from **Matthew 22:36-40**.

1. **Reflect on Your Meditations**:
   Recall the reflections and insights from your meditation

on Matthew 22:36-40.

2. **Begin with Praise and Thanksgiving**:
"Lord, I praise You for Your wisdom and Your commandments that guide us. Thank You for teaching us the greatest commandments of loving You and loving our neighbours."

3. **Confession and Requests**:
"Father, I confess that I often fall short in loving You with all my heart, soul, and mind. Help me to deepen my love for You and make it more wholehearted."

"Jesus, I struggle with loving certain neighbours as myself. Give me the grace and strength to love them as You love me."

4. **Listening for God's Response**:
After speaking these prayers, sit in silence. Be attentive to any thoughts or feelings that may arise. These could be God's way of responding to your prayers.

5. **Conclude with a Surrender**:
"Lord, I surrender these prayers to You. Help me to live out Your commandments in my daily life. Guide me, teach me, and mould my heart according to Your will. Amen."

Concluding Oratio

After your prayer time, take a moment to reflect on the experience. Note any significant feelings, thoughts, or responses that occurred. Thank God for the time spent in prayer and for His presence with you. This prepares you for the final step of

Lectio Divina: Contemplatio (Contemplate), where you will rest in God's presence and embrace His love and guidance.

5

Contemplatio

In peace I will both lay myself down and sleep, for you, Yahweh alone, make me live in safety.
Psalm 4:8

Contemplate: Rest in These Thoughts and Prayers

Contemplatio is the fourth and final step in the Lectio Divina practice, following *Lectio* (Read), *Meditatio* (Meditate), and *Oratio* (Pray). After reading the scripture, reflecting on its meaning, and conversing with God in prayer, we now move into a time of quiet contemplation. *Contemplatio* invites us to rest in God's presence, allowing the insights and prayers to sink deeply into our hearts and minds. This step is about letting go and being open to the Holy Spirit's work within us.

Preparing for Contemplatio

1. **Find a Quiet Space**: Choose a place where you can sit comfortably and undisturbed. A peaceful environment helps foster a sense of stillness and receptivity.
2. **Calm Your Mind and Body**: Take a few deep breaths to relax and centre yourself. Let go of any distractions or concerns that might interfere with your focus.
3. **Invite the Holy Spirit**: Begin with a simple prayer inviting the Holy Spirit to guide and deepen your time of contemplation. Ask for an open heart and mind to receive God's presence. To do this you can say your own prayer, or use one of the following *invitatory prayers* from traditional liturgy:

   "O God lead us from death to life, from falsehood to truth. Lead us from despair to hope, from fear to trust. Lead us from hate to love, from war to peace. Let your peace that passes understanding fill our hearts and our world."

   "O God make speed to save me, O Lord make haste to help me, Glory to the Father, and to the Son, and to the Holy Spirit: As it was in the beginning, is now, and will be forever. Amen."

The Process of Contemplatio

1. **Rest in God's Presence**: Close your eyes and focus on the presence of God. Allow yourself to simply be with Him, without the need for words or active thoughts. Trust that God is with you, loving you and working within you.
2. **Let Go of Active Thought**: Unlike *Meditatio*, where you

actively reflect on the text, *Contemplatio* involves releasing your thoughts and just being. If your mind starts to wander, gently bring your focus back to God's presence.

3. **Be Receptive to the Holy Spirit**: Open your heart to the Holy Spirit's work. You might not feel anything dramatic, but trust that God is at work within you, bringing peace, healing, and deeper understanding.

4. **Embrace Silence**: Embrace the silence as a sacred space where God speaks to you in ways beyond words. This silence is not empty but filled with God's presence and love.

Tools for Deeper Contemplation

1. **Use a Sacred Word or Phrase**: Choose a word or phrase that helps centre your mind on God, such as "peace," "love," or "Jesus." Repeat it silently to yourself whenever you feel your mind wandering. You could also pray the short and simple "Jesus Prayer" to refocus: *Lord Jesus Christ, Son of God, have mercy on me, a sinner.*

2. **Focus on Your Breath**: Pay attention to your breathing as a way to stay present and connected to the moment. Let each breath remind you of God's life-giving presence.

3. **Visualisation**: Imagine yourself in a peaceful, serene place where you feel close to God. This can help you enter into a deeper state of contemplation.

4. **Gentle Music or Nature Sounds**: Soft background music or nature sounds can aid in creating a calming atmosphere conducive to contemplation.

Practical Example

Let's continue with the passage from **Matthew 22:36-40**.

1. **Reflect Briefly on the Passage**: Recall the essence of Matthew 22:36-40:
   "Teacher, which is the greatest commandment in the Law?" Jesus replied: "'Love the Lord your God with all your heart and with all your soul and with all your mind.' This is the first and greatest commandment. And the second is like it: 'Love your neighbour as yourself.' All the Law and the Prophets hang on these two commandments."

2. **Rest in the Love of God**:
   Close your eyes and imagine God's love surrounding you. Feel His presence enveloping you in warmth and peace.

3. **Let Go of Words**:
   Release any active thoughts or concerns. If a thought arises, acknowledge it and then gently let it go, returning your focus to God's presence.

4. **Be Open to the Holy Spirit**:
   Sit quietly, allowing the Holy Spirit to work within you. Trust that in this silence, God is speaking to your heart in profound ways.

5. **Embrace the Silence**:
   Embrace the quiet, knowing it is filled with God's love and presence. Rest in the stillness, allowing God's peace to fill your soul.

Concluding Contemplatio

After your time of contemplation, gently bring your awareness back to your surroundings. Take a moment to reflect on the experience and thank God for His presence and the work He is doing in your life. This step completes the cycle of *Lectio Divina*, leaving you refreshed and spiritually nourished.

Now, you can move into the next section of the book and apply the methods you have learned here to the verses of Scripture that focus on your heart, soul, mind, strength, and loving your neighbour. Be mindful of the Holy Spirit's guidance and leading in these areas of your life.

II

The Scripture

This book is structured into five sections: Heart, Soul, Mind, Strength, and Love Your Neighbour. Each section compiles relevant Bible verses related to its theme, such as worship and character for the Heart section. Using the Lectio Divina method, you'll read these verses, identify the one that speaks to you, and then pray and meditate on it.

These sections also will help you focus on the areas in your life needing growth, aiding you in living out the Greatest Commandment in all its fullness.

6

All Your Heart

We start with the *heart.* The heart is a tricky thing that can be the cause of much turmoil in our lives, emotionally speaking. The Bible talks a lot about our heart, both in positive and negative ways which makes discerning how we feel and think of the upmost importance. This chapter begins with a verse which I was unsure whether to include, especially as the opening text, since it is quite negative. But I decided to keep it as it really sets the tone of the human condition and highlights precisely *why* we must incline our hearts towards God continuously, because without Him, we will fall back into corruption.

Read through these verses, but don't *just* read—pray at the same time and let the Holy Spirit lead you and speak to you through the Scriptures about your own heart condition.

* * *

Old Testament

Genesis

Genesis 6:5
Yahweh saw that the wickedness of man was great in the earth, and that every imagination of the thoughts of man's heart was continually only evil.

* * *

Leviticus

Leviticus 19:17
You shall not hate your brother in your heart. You shall surely rebuke your neighbour, and not bear sin because of him.

* * *

Deuteronomy

Deuteronomy 4:29
From there you will seek the Lord your God, and you will find him if you search after him with all your heart and soul.

Deuteronomy 4:39
Know therefore today, and take it to heart, that Yahweh himself is God in heaven above and on the earth beneath. There is no one else.

Deuteronomy 5:29

Oh that there were such a heart in them that they would fear me and keep all my commandments always, that it might be well with them and with their children forever!

Deuteronomy 6:5-7

You shall love Yahweh your God with all your heart, with all your soul, and with all your might. These words, which I command you today, shall be on your heart; and you shall teach them diligently to your children, and shall talk of them when you sit in your house, and when you walk by the way, and when you lie down, and when you rise up.

Deuteronomy 8:5

You shall consider in your heart that as a man disciplines his son, so Yahweh your God disciplines you.

Deuteronomy 10:12, 13

Now, Israel, what does Yahweh your God require of you, but to fear Yahweh your God, to walk in all his ways, to love him, and to serve Yahweh your God with all your heart and with all your soul, to keep Yahweh's commandments and statutes, which I command you today for your good?

Deuteronomy 10:16, 17

Circumcise therefore the foreskin of your heart, and be no more stiff-necked. For Yahweh your God, he is God of gods and Lord of lords, the great God, the mighty, and the awesome, who doesn't respect persons or take bribes.

Deuteronomy 11:13, 14

It shall happen, if you shall listen diligently to my commandments which I command you today, to love Yahweh your God, and to serve him with all your heart and with all your soul, **14** that I will give the rain for your land in its season, the early rain and the latter rain, that you may gather in your grain, your new wine, and your oil.

Deuteronomy 11:16

Be careful, lest your heart be deceived, and you turn away to serve other gods and worship them...

Deuteronomy 11:18

Therefore you shall lay up these words of mine in your heart and in your soul. You shall bind them for a sign on your hand, and they shall be for frontlets between your eyes.

Deuteronomy 26:16

Today Yahweh your God commands you to do these statutes and ordinances. You shall therefore keep and do them with all your heart and with all your soul.

Deuteronomy 30:6

Yahweh your God will circumcise your heart, and the heart of your offspring, to love Yahweh your God with all your heart and with all your soul, that you may live.

Deuteronomy 30:14

But the word is very near to you, in your mouth and in your heart, that you may do it.

* * *

Joshua

Joshua 22:5

Only take diligent heed to do the commandment and the law which Moses the servant of Yahweh commanded you, to love Yahweh your God, to walk in all his ways, to keep his commandments, to hold fast to him, and to serve him with all your heart and with all your soul.

Joshua 24:23

Now therefore put away the foreign gods which are among you, and incline your heart to Yahweh, the God of Israel.

* * *

1 Samuel

1 Samuel 2:1

Hannah prayed, and said: "My heart exults in Yahweh! My horn is exalted in Yahweh. My mouth is enlarged over my enemies, because I rejoice in your salvation."

1 Samuel 12:24

Only fear Yahweh, and serve him in truth with all your heart; for consider what great things he has done for you.

* * *

1 Kings

1 Kings 8:23

and he said, "Yahweh, the God of Israel, there is no God like you, in heaven above, or on earth beneath; who keeps covenant and loving kindness with your servants, who walk before you with all their heart..."

1 Kings 8:57-58

May Yahweh our God be with us, as he was with our fathers. Let him not leave us or forsake us; that he may incline our hearts to him, to walk in all his ways, and to keep his commandments, and his statutes, and his ordinances, which he commanded our fathers.

* * *

1 Chronicles

1 Chronicles 16:10

Glory in his holy name. Let the heart of those who seek Yahweh rejoice.

1 Chronicles 22:19

Now set your heart and your soul to follow Yahweh your God.

1 Chronicles 28:9

...for Yahweh searches all hearts, and understands all the imaginations of the thoughts. If you seek him, he will be found by you; but if you forsake him, he will cast you off forever.

1 Chronicles 29:17

I know also, my God, that you try the heart, and have pleasure in uprightness. As for me, in the uprightness of my heart I have willingly offered all these things. Now I have seen with joy your people, who are present here, offer willingly to you.

* * *

2 Chronicles

2 Chronicles 16:9

For Yahweh's eyes run back and forth throughout the whole earth, to show himself strong in the behalf of them whose heart is perfect toward him. You have done foolishly in this; for from now on you will have wars.

2 Chronicles 25:2

He did that which was right in Yahweh's eyes, but not with a perfect heart.

2 Chronicles 29:10

Now it is in my heart to make a covenant with Yahweh, the God of Israel, that his fierce anger may turn away from us.

* * *

Psalms

Psalm 4:4
Stand in awe, and don't sin. Search your own heart on your bed, and be still.

Psalm 4:7
You have put gladness in my heart, more than when their grain and their new wine are increased.

Psalm 7:9
Oh let the wickedness of the wicked come to an end, but establish the righteous; their minds and hearts are searched by the righteous God.

Psalm 7:10
My shield is with God, who saves the upright in heart.

Psalm 9:1
I will give thanks to Yahweh with my whole heart. I will tell of all your marvellous works.

Psalm 10:17, 18
Yahweh, you have heard the desire of the humble. You will prepare their heart. You will cause your ear to hear, to judge the fatherless and the oppressed, that man who is of the earth may terrify no more.

Psalm 13:5
But I trust in your loving kindness. My heart rejoices in your salvation.

Psalm 15:1-3

Yahweh, who shall dwell in your sanctuary? Who shall live on your holy hill? He who walks blamelessly and does what is right, and speaks truth in his heart; he who doesn't slander with his tongue, nor does evil to his friend, nor casts slurs against his fellow man...

Psalm 16:7-9

I will bless Yahweh, who has given me counsel. Yes, my heart instructs me in the night seasons. I have set Yahweh always before me. Because he is at my right hand, I shall not be moved. Therefore my heart is glad, and my tongue rejoices. My body shall also dwell in safety.

Psalm 17:3

You have proved my heart. You have visited me in the night. You have tried me, and found nothing. I have resolved that my mouth shall not disobey.

Psalm 19:8

Yahweh's precepts are right, rejoicing the heart. Yahweh's commandment is pure, enlightening the eyes.

Psalm 19:14

Let the words of my mouth and the meditation of my heart be acceptable in your sight, Yahweh, my rock, and my redeemer.

Psalm 20:4

May he grant you your heart's desire, and fulfil all your counsel.

Psalm 22:14

I am poured out like water. All my bones are out of joint. My heart is like wax. It is melted within me.

Psalm 22:26

The humble shall eat and be satisfied. They shall praise Yahweh who seek after him. Let your hearts live forever.

Psalm 24:3-5

Who may ascend to Yahweh's hill? Who may stand in his holy place? He who has clean hands and a pure heart; who has not lifted up his soul to falsehood, and has not sworn deceitfully. He shall receive a blessing from Yahweh, righteousness from the God of his salvation.

Psalm 25:17

The troubles of my heart are enlarged. Oh bring me out of my distresses.

Psalm 26:2

Examine me, Yahweh, and prove me. Try my heart and my mind.

Psalm 27:3

Though an army should encamp against me, my heart shall not fear. Though war should rise against me, even then I will be confident.

Psalm 27:8

When you said, "Seek my face," my heart said to you, "I will seek your face, Yahweh."

Psalm 27:14

Wait for Yahweh. Be strong, and let your heart take courage. Yes, wait for Yahweh.

Psalm 28:7

Yahweh is my strength and my shield. My heart has trusted in him, and I am helped. Therefore my heart greatly rejoices. With my song I will thank him.

Psalm 31:24

Be strong, and let your heart take courage, all you who hope in Yahweh.

Psalm 32:11

Be glad in Yahweh, and rejoice, you righteous! Shout for joy, all you who are upright in heart!

Psalm 33:21

For our heart rejoices in him, because we have trusted in his holy name.

Psalm 34:18

Yahweh is near to those who have a broken heart, and saves those who have a crushed spirit.

Psalm 36:10

Oh continue your loving kindness to those who know you, your righteousness to the upright in heart.

Psalm 37:4

Also delight yourself in Yahweh, and he will give you the

desires of your heart.

Psalm 37:31
The law of his God is in his heart. None of his steps shall slide.

Psalm 38:8-10
I am faint and severely bruised. I have groaned by reason of the anguish of my heart. Lord, all my desire is before you. My groaning is not hidden from you. My heart throbs. My strength fails me. As for the light of my eyes, it has also left me.

Psalm 40:8-10
I delight to do your will, my God. Yes, your law is within my heart. I have proclaimed glad news of righteousness in the great assembly. Behold, I will not seal my lips, Yahweh, you know. I have not hidden your righteousness within my heart. I have declared your faithfulness and your salvation. I have not concealed your loving kindness and your truth from the great assembly.

Psalm 44:18
Our heart has not turned back, neither have our steps strayed from your path...

Psalm 49:3
My mouth will speak words of wisdom. My heart will utter understanding.

Psalm 51:6
You desire truth in the inward being; therefore teach me wisdom in my secret heart.

Psalm 51:10

Create in me a clean heart, O God. Renew a right spirit within me.

Psalm 51:17

The sacrifices of God are a broken spirit. O God, you will not despise a broken and contrite heart.

Psalm 55:4

My heart is severely pained within me. The terrors of death have fallen on me.

Psalm 57:7

My heart is steadfast, God. My heart is steadfast. I will sing, yes, I will sing praises.

Psalm 61:1-3

Hear my cry, God. Listen to my prayer. From the end of the earth, I will call to you when my heart is overwhelmed. Lead me to the rock that is higher than I. For you have been a refuge for me, a strong tower from the enemy.

Psalm 62:8

Trust in him at all times, you people. Pour out your heart before him. God is a refuge for us.

Psalm 62:10

Don't trust in oppression. Don't become vain in robbery. If riches increase, don't set your heart on them.

Psalm 64:10

The righteous shall be glad in Yahweh, and shall take refuge in him. All the upright in heart shall praise him!

Psalm 66:18

If I cherished sin in my heart, the Lord wouldn't have listened.

Psalm 69:32

The humble have seen it, and are glad. You who seek after God, let your heart live.

Psalm 73:1

Surely God is good to Israel, to those who are pure in heart.

Psalm 73:26

My flesh and my heart fails, but God is the strength of my heart and my portion forever.

Psalm 84:2

My soul longs, and even faints for the courts of Yahweh. My heart and my flesh cry out for the living God.

Psalm 84:5

Blessed are those whose strength is in you, who have set their hearts on a pilgrimage.

Psalm 86:11

Teach me your way, Yahweh. I will walk in your truth. Make my heart undivided to fear your name.

Psalm 86:12

I will praise you, Lord my God, with my whole heart. I will

glorify your name forever more.

Psalm 90:12

So teach us to count our days, that we may gain a heart of wisdom.

Psalm 101:2-4

I will be careful to live a blameless life. When will you come to me? I will walk within my house with a blameless heart. I will set no vile thing before my eyes. I hate the deeds of faithless men. A perverse heart will be far from me. I will have nothing to do with evil.

Psalm 102:4

My heart is blighted like grass, and withered, for I forget to eat my bread.

Psalm 105:3

Glory in his holy name. Let the heart of those who seek Yahweh rejoice.

Psalm 108:1

My heart is steadfast, God. I will sing and I will make music with my soul.

Psalm 109:21,22

But deal with me, Yahweh the Lord, for your name's sake, because your loving kindness is good, deliver me; for I am poor and needy. My heart is wounded within me.

Psalm 111:1

Praise Yah! I will give thanks to Yahweh with my whole heart, in the council of the upright, and in the congregation.

Psalm 112:7

He will not be afraid of evil news. His heart is steadfast, trusting in Yahweh.

Psalm 119:2

Blessed are those who keep his statutes, who seek him with their whole heart.

Psalm 119:7

I will give thanks to you with uprightness of heart, when I learn your righteous judgments.

Psalm 119:10

With my whole heart, I have sought you. Don't let me wander from your commandments.

Psalm 119:11

I have hidden your word in my heart, that I might not sin against you.

Psalm 119:32

I run in the path of your commandments, for you have set my heart free.

Psalm 119:34

Give me understanding, and I will keep your law. Yes, I will obey it with my whole heart.

Psalm 119:36

Turn my heart toward your statutes, not toward selfish gain.

Psalm 119:58

I sought your favour with my whole heart. Be merciful to me according to your word.

Psalm 119:69

The proud have smeared a lie upon me. With my whole heart, I will keep your precepts.

Psalm 119:80

Let my heart be blameless toward your decrees, that I may not be disappointed.

Psalm 119:111

I have taken your testimonies as a heritage forever, for they are the joy of my heart.

Psalm 119:112

I have set my heart to perform your statutes forever, even to the end.

Psalm 119:145

I have called with my whole heart. Answer me, Yahweh! I will keep your statutes.

Psalm 119:161

Princes have persecuted me without a cause, but my heart stands in awe of your words.

Psalm 131:1

Yahweh, my heart isn't arrogant, nor my eyes lofty; nor do I concern myself with great matters, or things too wonderful for me.

Psalm 138:1

I will give you thanks with my whole heart. Before the gods, I will sing praises to you.

Psalm 139:23

Search me, God, and know my heart. Try me, and know my thoughts.

Psalm 143:4

Therefore my spirit is overwhelmed within me. My heart within me is desolate.

* * *

Proverbs

Proverbs 2:10

For wisdom will enter into your heart. Knowledge will be pleasant to your soul.

Proverbs 3:1-3

My son, don't forget my teaching; but let your heart keep my commandments: for they will add to you length of days, years of life, and peace. Don't let kindness and truth forsake you. Bind them around your neck. Write them on the tablet of your heart.

Proverbs 3:5
Trust in Yahweh with all your heart, and don't lean on your own understanding.

Proverbs 4:4
He taught me, and said to me: "Let your heart retain my words. Keep my commandments, and live."

Proverbs 4:23
Keep your heart with all diligence, for out of it is the wellspring of life.

Proverbs 10:8
The wise in heart accept commandments, but a chattering fool will fall.

Proverbs 12:25
Anxiety in a man's heart weighs it down, but a kind word makes it glad.

Proverbs 14:10
The heart knows its own bitterness and joy; he will not share these with a stranger.

Proverbs 14:13
Even in laughter the heart may be sorrowful, and mirth may end in heaviness.

Proverbs 14:30

The life of the body is a heart at peace, but envy rots the bones.

Proverbs 14:33

Wisdom rests in the heart of one who has understanding, and is even made known in the inward part of fools.

Proverbs 15:13

A glad heart makes a cheerful face, but an aching heart breaks the spirit.

Proverbs 15:28

The heart of the righteous weighs answers, but the mouth of the wicked gushes out evil.

Proverbs 16:1

The plans of the heart belong to man, but the answer of the tongue is from Yahweh.

Proverbs 16:5

Everyone who is proud in heart is an abomination to Yahweh: they shall certainly not be unpunished.

Proverbs 16:9

A man's heart plans his course, but Yahweh directs his steps.

Proverbs 16:23

The heart of the wise instructs his mouth, and adds learning to his lips.

Proverbs 17:22

A cheerful heart makes good medicine, but a crushed spirit

dries up the bones.

Proverbs 18:15
The heart of the discerning gets knowledge. The ear of the wise seeks knowledge.

Proverbs 23:12
Apply your heart to instruction, and your ears to the words of knowledge.

Proverbs 23:17
Don't let your heart envy sinners, but rather fear Yahweh all day long.

Proverbs 24:17
Don't rejoice when your enemy falls. Don't let your heart be glad when he is overthrown

Proverbs 27:19
Like water reflects a face, so a man's heart reflects the man.

Proverbs 28:14
Blessed is the man who always fears; but one who hardens his heart falls into trouble.

* * *

Ecclesiastes

Ecclesiastes 1:17

I applied my heart to know wisdom, and to know madness and folly. I perceived that this also was a chasing after wind.

Ecclesiastes 2:1

I said in my heart, "Come now, I will test you with mirth: therefore enjoy pleasure;" and behold, this also was vanity.

Ecclesiastes 5:2

Don't be rash with your mouth, and don't let your heart be hasty to utter anything before God; for God is in heaven, and you on earth. Therefore let your words be few.

Ecclesiastes 7:22

...for often your own heart knows that you yourself have likewise cursed others.

Ecclesiastes 10:2

A wise man's heart is at his right hand, but a fool's heart at his left.

Ecclesiastes 11:10

Therefore remove sorrow from your heart, and put away evil from your flesh; for youth and the dawn of life are vanity.

* * *

Isaiah

Isaiah 21:4

My heart flutters. Horror has frightened me. The twilight that I desired has been turned into trembling for me.

* * *

Jeremiah

Jeremiah 8:18

Oh that I could comfort myself against sorrow! My heart is faint within me.

Jeremiah 17:9

The heart is deceitful above all things and it is exceedingly corrupt. Who can know it?

Jeremiah 29:13

You shall seek me, and find me, when you search for me with all your heart.

Jeremiah 51:46

Don't let your heart faint. Don't fear for the news that will be heard in the land. For news will come one year, and after that in another year news will come, and violence in the land, ruler against ruler.

* * *

Lamentations

Lamentations 1:20

"Look, Yahweh; for I am in distress. My heart is troubled. My heart turns over within me, for I have grievously rebelled. Abroad, the sword bereaves. At home, it is like death."

Lamentations 2:18

Their heart cried to the Lord. O wall of the daughter of Zion, let tears run down like a river day and night. Give yourself no relief. Don't let your eyes rest.

Lamentations 3:41

Let's lift up our heart with our hands to God in the heavens.

Lamentations 5:15

The joy of our heart has ceased. Our dance is turned into mourning.

* * *

Ezekiel

Ezekiel 3:10

Moreover he said to me, "Son of man, receive in your heart and hear with your ears all my words that I speak to you."

Ezekiel 22:14

Can your heart endure, or can your hands be strong, in the days that I will deal with you? I, Yahweh, have spoken it, and will do it.

Ezekiel 36:26

I will also give you a new heart, and I will put a new spirit within you. I will take away the stony heart out of your flesh, and I will give you a heart of flesh.

* * *

Joel

Joel 2:12-13

"Yet even now," says Yahweh, "turn to me with all your heart, and with fasting, and with weeping, and with mourning." Tear your heart, and not your garments, and turn to Yahweh, your God; for he is gracious and merciful, slow to anger, and abundant in loving kindness, and relents from sending calamity.

* * *

Zechariah

Zechariah 7:10

Don't oppress the widow, nor the fatherless, the foreigner, nor the poor; and let none of you devise evil against his brother in your heart.

* * *

New Testament

Matthew

Matthew 5:8

Blessed are the pure in heart, for they shall see God.

Matthew 5:28

...but I tell you that everyone who gazes at a woman to lust after her has committed adultery with her already in his heart.

Matthew 6:21

...for where your treasure is, there your heart will be also.

Matthew 15:18, 19

But the things which proceed out of the mouth come out of the heart, and they defile the man. For out of the heart come evil thoughts, murders, adulteries, sexual sins, thefts, false testimony, and blasphemies.

Matthew 18:34, 35

His lord was angry, and delivered him to the tormentors until he should pay all that was due to him. So my heavenly Father will also do to you, if you don't each forgive your brother from your hearts for his misdeeds.

Matthew 22:37

Jesus said to him, "'You shall love the Lord your God with all your heart, with all your soul, and with all your mind.'"

Mark

Mark 7:20-22

He said, "That which proceeds out of the man, that defiles the man. For from within, out of the hearts of men, proceed evil thoughts, adulteries, sexual sins, murders, thefts, covetings, wickedness, deceit, lustful desires, an evil eye, blasphemy, pride, and foolishness.

Mark 11:23

For most certainly I tell you, whoever may tell this mountain, 'Be taken up and cast into the sea,' and doesn't doubt in his heart, but believes that what he says is happening; he shall have whatever he says.

Mark 12:29-31

Jesus answered, "The greatest is, 'Hear, Israel, the Lord our God, the Lord is one: 30 you shall love the Lord your God with all your heart, and with all your soul, and with all your mind, and with all your strength.' This is the first commandment. The second is like this, 'You shall love your neighbour as yourself.' There is no other commandment greater than these."

Luke

Luke 6:45

The good man out of the good treasure of his heart brings out that which is good, and the evil man out of the evil treasure of his heart brings out that which is evil, for out of the abundance of the heart, his mouth speaks.

Luke 10:27
He answered, "You shall love the Lord your God with all your heart, with all your soul, with all your strength, and with all your mind; and your neighbour as yourself."

Luke 12:34
For where your treasure is, there will your heart be also.

Luke 21:14, 15
Settle it therefore in your hearts not to meditate beforehand how to answer, for I will give you a mouth and wisdom which all your adversaries will not be able to withstand or to contradict.

Luke 21:34-36
"So be careful, or your hearts will be loaded down with carousing, drunkenness, and cares of this life, and that day will come on you suddenly. For it will come like a snare on all those who dwell on the surface of all the earth. Therefore be watchful all the time, praying that you may be counted worthy to escape all these things that will happen, and to stand before the Son of Man."

John

John 14:1
"Don't let your heart be troubled. Believe in God. Believe also in me."

John 14:27

Peace I leave with you. My peace I give to you; not as the world gives, I give to you. Don't let your heart be troubled, neither let it be fearful.

Acts

Acts 2:46-47

Day by day, continuing steadfastly with one accord in the temple, and breaking bread at home, they took their food with gladness and singleness of heart, praising God, and having favour with all the people. The Lord added to the assembly day by day those who were being saved.

Acts 4:32

The multitude of those who believed were of one heart and soul. Not one of them claimed that anything of the things which he possessed was his own, but they had all things in common.

Romans

Romans 2:14-16

(for when Gentiles who don't have the law do by nature the things of the law, these, not having the law, are a law to themselves, in that they show the work of the law written in their hearts, their conscience testifying with them, and their thoughts among themselves accusing or else excusing them) in the day when God will judge the secrets of men, according to my Good News, by Jesus Christ.

Romans 2:29

...but he is a Jew who is one inwardly, and circumcision is that of the heart, in the spirit not in the letter; whose praise is not from men, but from God.

Romans 5:5

...and hope doesn't disappoint us, because God's love has been poured into our hearts through the Holy Spirit who was given to us.

Romans 6:17

But thanks be to God, that, whereas you were bondservants of sin, you became obedient from the heart to that form of teaching to which you were delivered.

Romans 8:27

He who searches the hearts knows what is on the Spirit's mind, because he makes intercession for the saints according to God.

Romans 10:8, 9

But what does it say? "The word is near you, in your mouth, and in your heart;" that is, the word of faith which we preach: that if you will confess with your mouth that Jesus is Lord, and believe in your heart that God raised him from the dead, you will be saved.

Romans 10:10

For with the heart, one believes resulting in righteousness; and with the mouth confession is made resulting in salvation.

1 Corinthians

1 Corinthians 2:9
But as it is written, "Things which an eye didn't see, and an ear didn't hear, which didn't enter into the heart of man, these God has prepared for those who love him."

1 Corinthians 4:5
Therefore judge nothing before the time, until the Lord comes, who will both bring to light the hidden things of darkness, and reveal the counsels of the hearts. Then each man will get his praise from God.

1 Corinthians 7:37
But he who stands steadfast in his heart, having no urgency, but has power over his own will, and has determined in his own heart to keep his own virgin, does well.

2 Corinthians 9:7
Let each man give according as he has determined in his heart, not grudgingly or under compulsion, for God loves a cheerful giver.

Galatians

Galatians 4:6
And because you are children, God sent out the Spirit of his Son into your hearts, crying, "Abba, Father!"

Ephesians

Ephesians 1:18
...having the eyes of your hearts enlightened, that you may know what is the hope of his calling, and what are the riches of the glory of his inheritance in the saints...

Ephesians 3:17-19
...that Christ may dwell in your hearts through faith, to the end that you, being rooted and grounded in love, may be strengthened to comprehend with all the saints what is the width and length and height and depth, and to know Christ's love which surpasses knowledge, that you may be filled with all the fullness of God.

Ephesians 5:18,19
Don't be drunken with wine, in which is dissipation, but be filled with the Spirit, speaking to one another in psalms, hymns, and spiritual songs; singing and making melody in your heart to the Lord

Philippians

Philippians 4:7
And the peace of God, which surpasses all understanding, will guard your hearts and your thoughts in Christ Jesus.

Colossians

Colossians 3:12-16

Put on therefore, as God's chosen ones, holy and beloved, a heart of compassion, kindness, lowliness, humility, and perseverance; bearing with one another, and forgiving each other, if any man has a complaint against any; even as Christ forgave you, so you also do. Above all these things, walk in love, which is the bond of perfection. And let the peace of God rule in your hearts, to which also you were called in one body, and be thankful. Let the word of Christ dwell in you richly; in all wisdom teaching and admonishing one another with psalms, hymns, and spiritual songs, singing with grace in your heart to the Lord.

2 Thessalonians

2 Thessalonians 2:16-17

Now our Lord Jesus Christ himself, and God our Father, who loved us and gave us eternal comfort and good hope through grace, comfort your hearts and establish you in every good work and word.

2 Thessalonians 3:5

May the Lord direct your hearts into God's love, and into the perseverance of Christ.

1 Timothy

1 Timothy 1:5

...but the goal of this command is love, out of a pure heart and a good conscience and sincere faith...

2 Timothy

2 Timothy 2:22

Flee from youthful lusts; but pursue righteousness, faith, love, and peace with those who call on the Lord out of a pure heart.

Hebrews

Hebrews 3:12, 13

Beware, brothers, lest perhaps there might be in any one of you an evil heart of unbelief, in falling away from the living God; but exhort one another day by day, so long as it is called "today", lest any one of you be hardened by the deceitfulness of sin.

Hebrews 4:12

For the word of God is living and active, and sharper than any two-edged sword, piercing even to the dividing of soul and spirit, of both joints and marrow, and is able to discern the thoughts and intentions of the heart.

Hebrews 10:22, 23

...let's draw near with a true heart in fullness of faith, having our hearts sprinkled from an evil conscience, and having our body washed with pure water, let's hold fast the confession of our hope without wavering; for he who promised is faithful.

Hebrews 13:9

Don't be carried away by various and strange teachings, for it is good that the heart be established by grace, not by food, through which those who were so occupied were not benefited.

James

James 1:26

If anyone among you thinks himself to be religious while he doesn't bridle his tongue, but deceives his heart, this man's religion is worthless.

James 3:14

But if you have bitter jealousy and selfish ambition in your heart, don't boast and don't lie against the truth.

James 4:8

Draw near to God, and he will draw near to you. Cleanse your hands, you sinners. Purify your hearts, you double-minded.

James 5:8

You also be patient. Establish your hearts, for the coming of the Lord is at hand.

1 Peter

1 Peter 1:22, 23

Seeing you have purified your souls in your obedience to the truth through the Spirit in sincere brotherly affection, love one another from the heart fervently, having been born again, not of corruptible seed, but of incorruptible, through the word of God, which lives and remains forever.

1 Peter 3:15, 16

But sanctify the Lord God in your hearts. Always be ready to give an answer to everyone who asks you a reason concerning the hope that is in you, with humility and fear, having a good conscience.

1 John

1 John 3:17

But whoever has the world's goods and sees his brother in need, then closes his heart of compassion against him, how does God's love remain in him?

1 John 3:19-21

And by this we know that we are of the truth, and persuade our hearts before him, because if our heart condemns us, God is greater than our heart, and knows all things. Beloved, if our hearts don't condemn us, we have boldness toward God...

7

All Your Soul

The Soul. What *is* the soul? A question that has provoked many discussions over the centuries, often turning it into the metaphysical *inner-man* that is sometime separate from our body of flesh.

The Hebrew word is נֶפֶשׁ **nephesh** and it generally means: *a breathing creature, i.e. animal of (abstractly) vitality; used very widely in a literal, accommodated or figurative sense (bodily or mental)*, according to Strong's Concordance.[1] From this we can deduce the meaning in the ancient Hebrew mind was more *wholistic* than our modern thinking can be, and viewed a "soul" as the whole, living person, not necessarily just a spiritual part within. This becomes clearer when we read the creation story, which is the verse we begin with in this chapter.

So with this in mind, consider the following verses in a more wholistic, bodily, *and* spiritual sense—your whole being and self which we must give to God (Romans 12:1, c.f. 1 Peter 2:5).

---

[1] Carlton, D. (2022) *Strong's Concordance.* Available at: https://strongsconcor dance.org/ (Accessed: 06 June 2024).

Read through these verses, but don't *just* read—pray at the same time and let the Holy Spirit lead you and speak to you through the Scriptures about how you can present your whole being—your soul—to God, and also *be* present with your whole self before God, like the example we see from David in the Psalms.

* * *

Old Testament

Genesis

Genesis 2:7

Yahweh God formed man from the dust of the ground, and breathed into his nostrils the breath of life; and man became a living soul.

* * *

Leviticus

Leviticus 16:31

It is a Sabbath of solemn rest to you, and you shall afflict your souls. It is a statute forever.

* * *

Numbers

Numbers 30:2

When a man vows a vow to Yahweh, or swears an oath to bind his soul with a bond, he shall not break his word. He shall do according to all that proceeds out of his mouth.

* * *

Deuteronomy

Deuteronomy 4:29

But from there you shall seek Yahweh your God, and you will find him when you search after him with all your heart and with all your soul.

Deuteronomy 6:5

You shall love Yahweh your God with all your heart, with all your soul, and with all your might.

Deuteronomy 10:12, 13

Now, Israel, what does Yahweh your God require of you, but to fear Yahweh your God, to walk in all his ways, to love him, and to serve Yahweh your God with all your heart and with all your soul, to keep Yahweh's commandments and statutes, which I command you today for your good?

Deuteronomy 11:18

Therefore you shall lay up these words of mine in your heart and in your soul. You shall bind them for a sign on your hand,

and they shall be for frontlets between your eyes.

Deuteronomy 26:16

Today Yahweh your God commands you to do these statutes and ordinances. You shall therefore keep and do them with all your heart and with all your soul.

Deuteronomy 30:6

Yahweh your God will circumcise your heart, and the heart of your offspring, to love Yahweh your God with all your heart and with all your soul, that you may live.

Deuteronomy 30:9, 10

Yahweh your God will make you prosperous in all the work of your hand, in the fruit of your body, in the fruit of your livestock, and in the fruit of your ground, for good; for Yahweh will again rejoice over you for good, as he rejoiced over your fathers, if you will obey Yahweh your God's voice, to keep his commandments and his statutes which are written in this book of the law; if you turn to Yahweh your God with all your heart and with all your soul.

* * *

1 Chronicles

1 Chronicles 22:19

Now set your heart and your soul to follow Yahweh your God.

* * *

Job

Job 7:11

Therefore I will not keep silent. I will speak in the anguish of my spirit. I will complain in the bitterness of my soul.

Job 10:1

My soul is weary of my life. I will give free course to my complaint. I will speak in the bitterness of my soul.

Job 30:16

Now my soul is poured out within me. Days of affliction have taken hold of me.

Job 30:25

Didn't I weep for him who was in trouble? Wasn't my soul grieved for the needy?

Job 33:28

He has redeemed my soul from going into the pit. My life will see the light.

* * *

Psalms

Psalm 6:3, 4

My soul is also in great anguish. But you, Yahweh—how long? Return, Yahweh. Deliver my soul, and save me for your loving kindness' sake.

Psalm 11:1

In Yahweh, I take refuge. How can you say to my soul, "Flee as a bird to your mountain"?

Psalm 13:2

How long shall I take counsel in my soul, having sorrow in my heart every day? How long shall my enemy triumph over me?

Psalm 16:2

My soul, you have said to Yahweh, "You are my Lord. Apart from you I have no good thing."

Psalm 19:7

Yahweh's law is perfect, restoring the soul. Yahweh's covenant is sure, making wise the simple.

Psalm 22:20

Deliver my soul from the sword, my precious life from the power of the dog.

Psalm 23:3

He restores my soul. He guides me in the paths of righteousness for his name's sake.

Psalm 24:3-5

Who may ascend to Yahweh's hill? Who may stand in his holy place? He who has clean hands and a pure heart; who has not lifted up his soul to falsehood, and has not sworn deceitfully. He shall receive a blessing from Yahweh, righteousness from the God of his salvation.

Psalm 25:1

To you, Yahweh, I lift up my soul.

Psalm 25:12-14

What man is he who fears Yahweh? He shall instruct him in the way that he shall choose. His soul will dwell at ease. His offspring will inherit the land. The friendship of Yahweh is with those who fear him. He will show them his covenant.

Psalm 25:20

Oh keep my soul, and deliver me. Let me not be disappointed, for I take refuge in you.

Psalm 26:8, 9

Yahweh, I love the habitation of your house, the place where your glory dwells. Don't gather my soul with sinners, nor my life with bloodthirsty men...

Psalm 30:2, 3

Yahweh my God, I cried to you, and you have healed me. Yahweh, you have brought up my soul from Sheol. You have kept me alive, that I should not go down to the pit.

Psalm 31:7

I will be glad and rejoice in your loving kindness, for you have seen my affliction. You have known my soul in adversities.

Psalm 31:9

Have mercy on me, Yahweh, for I am in distress. My eye, my soul, and my body waste away with grief.

Psalm 33:20

Our soul has waited for Yahweh. He is our help and our shield.

Psalm 34:2

My soul shall boast in Yahweh. The humble shall hear of it and be glad.

Psalm 34:22

Yahweh redeems the soul of his servants. None of those who take refuge in him shall be condemned.

Psalm 35:9

My soul shall be joyful in Yahweh. It shall rejoice in his salvation.

Psalm 35:12

They reward me evil for good, to the bereaving of my soul.

Psalm 35:13

But as for me, when they were sick, my clothing was sackcloth. I afflicted my soul with fasting. My prayer returned into my own bosom.

Psalm 35:17

Lord, how long will you look on? Rescue my soul from their destruction, my precious life from the lions.

Psalm 42:1, 2

As the deer pants for the water brooks, so my soul pants after you, God. My soul thirsts for God, for the living God. When shall I come and appear before God?

Psalm 42:5

Why are you in despair, my soul? Why are you disturbed within me? Hope in God! For I shall still praise him for the saving help of his presence.

Psalm 43:5

Why are you in despair, my soul? Why are you disturbed within me? Hope in God! For I shall still praise him: my Saviour, my helper, and my God.

Psalm 44:25, 26

For our soul is bowed down to the dust. Our body clings to the earth. Rise up to help us.

Redeem us for your loving kindness' sake.

Psalm 49:15

But God will redeem my soul from the power of Sheol, for he will receive me.

Psalm 54:4

Behold, God is my helper. The Lord is the one who sustains my soul.

Psalm 55:18

He has redeemed my soul in peace from the battle that was against me, although there are many who oppose me.

Psalm 56:13

For you have delivered my soul from death, and prevented my feet from falling, that I may walk before God in the light of the living.

Psalm 57:1

Be merciful to me, God, be merciful to me, for my soul takes refuge in you. Yes, in the shadow of your wings, I will take refuge, until disaster has passed.

Psalm 59:3

For, behold, they lie in wait for my soul. The mighty gather themselves together against me, not for my disobedience, nor for my sin, Yahweh.

Psalm 62:1

My soul rests in God alone. My salvation is from him.

Psalm 62:5

My soul, wait in silence for God alone, for my expectation is from him

Psalm 63:1

God, you are my God. I will earnestly seek you. My soul thirsts for you. My flesh longs for you, in a dry and weary land, where there is no water.

Psalm 63:8

My soul stays close to you. Your right hand holds me up.

Psalm 66:16

Come and hear, all you who fear God. I will declare what he has done for my soul.

Psalm 69:18

Draw near to my soul and redeem it. Ransom me because of

my enemies.

Psalm 71:23

My lips shall shout for joy! My soul, which you have redeemed, sings praises to you!

Psalm 73:21

For my soul was grieved. I was embittered in my heart.

Psalm 77:2

In the day of my trouble I sought the Lord. My hand was stretched out in the night, and didn't get tired. My soul refused to be comforted.

Psalm 84:2

My soul longs, and even faints for the courts of Yahweh. My heart and my flesh cry out for the living God.

Psalm 86:2-4

Preserve my soul, for I am godly. You, my God, save your servant who trusts in you. Be merciful to me, Lord, for I call to you all day long. Bring joy to the soul of your servant, for to you, Lord, do I lift up my soul.

Psalm 86:13

For your loving kindness is great toward me. You have delivered my soul from the lowest Sheol.

Psalm 88:3

For my soul is full of troubles. My life draws near to Sheol.

Psalm 88:14

Yahweh, why do you reject my soul? Why do you hide your face from me?

Psalm 89:48

What man is he who shall live and not see death, who shall deliver his soul from the power of Sheol?

Psalm 94:17

Unless Yahweh had been my help, my soul would have soon lived in silence.

Psalm 94:19

In the multitude of my thoughts within me, your comforts delight my soul.

Psalm 97:10

You who love Yahweh, hate evil! He preserves the souls of his saints. He delivers them out of the hand of the wicked.

Psalm 103:1-5

Praise Yahweh, my soul! All that is within me, praise his holy name! Praise Yahweh, my soul, and don't forget all his benefits, who forgives all your sins, who heals all your diseases, who redeems your life from destruction, who crowns you with loving kindness and tender mercies, who satisfies your desire with good things, so that your youth is renewed like the eagle's.

Psalm 103:22

Praise Yahweh, all you works of his, in all places of his dominion. Praise Yahweh, my soul!

Psalm 104:1

Bless Yahweh, my soul. Yahweh, my God, you are very great. You are clothed with honour and majesty.

Psalm 104:35

Let sinners be consumed out of the earth. Let the wicked be no more. Bless Yahweh, my soul. Praise Yah!

Psalm 107:9

For he satisfies the longing soul. He fills the hungry soul with good.

Psalm 108:1

My heart is steadfast, God. I will sing and I will make music with my soul.

Psalm 116:4, 8

Then I called on Yahweh's name: "Yahweh, I beg you, deliver my soul." ... For you have delivered my soul from death, my eyes from tears, and my feet from falling.

Psalm 119:20

My soul is consumed with longing for your ordinances at all times.

Psalm 119:25, 28

My soul is laid low in the dust. Revive me according to your word! ... My soul is weary with sorrow: strengthen me according to your word.

Psalm 119:81

My soul faints for your salvation. I hope in your word.

Psalm 119:109

My soul is continually in my hand, yet I won't forget your law.

Psalm 119:129

Your testimonies are wonderful, therefore my soul keeps them.

Psalm 119:167

My soul has observed your testimonies. I love them exceedingly.

Psalm 119:175

Let my soul live, that I may praise you. Let your ordinances help me.

Psalm 120:2

Deliver my soul, Yahweh, from lying lips, from a deceitful tongue.

Psalm 121:7

Yahweh will keep you from all evil. He will keep your soul.

Psalm 130:5

I wait for Yahweh. My soul waits. I hope in his word.

Psalm 130:6

My soul longs for the Lord more than watchmen long for the morning, more than watchmen for the morning.

Psalm 131:2

Surely I have stilled and quieted my soul, like a weaned child with his mother, like a weaned child is my soul within me.

Psalm 138:3

In the day that I called, you answered me. You encouraged me with strength in my soul.

Psalm 139:14

I will give thanks to you, for I am fearfully and wonderfully made. Your works are wonderful. My soul knows that very well.

Psalm 141:8

For my eyes are on you, Yahweh, the Lord. In you, I take refuge. Don't leave my soul destitute.

Psalm 143:6, 8, 11

I spread out my hands to you. My soul thirsts for you, like a parched land. ... Cause me to hear your loving kindness in the morning, for I trust in you. Cause me to know the way in which I should walk, for I lift up my soul to you. ... Revive me, Yahweh, for your name's sake. In your righteousness, bring my soul out of trouble.

Psalm 146:1

Praise Yah! Praise Yahweh, my soul.

* * *

Proverbs

Proverbs 2:10
For wisdom will enter into your heart. Knowledge will be pleasant to your soul.

Proverbs 3:21-23
My son, let them not depart from your eyes. Keep sound wisdom and discretion: so they will be life to your soul, and grace for your neck.

Proverbs 8:36
But he who sins against me wrongs his own soul. All those who hate me love death.

Proverbs 10:3
Yahweh will not allow the soul of the righteous to go hungry, but he thrusts away the desire of the wicked.

Proverbs 11:17
The merciful man does good to his own soul, but he who is cruel troubles his own flesh.

Proverbs 13:3
He who guards his mouth guards his soul. One who opens wide his lips comes to ruin.

Proverbs 13:19
Longing fulfilled is sweet to the soul, but fools detest turning from evil.

Proverbs 14:25
A truthful witness saves souls, but a false witness is deceitful.

Proverbs 15:32
He who refuses correction despises his own soul, but he who listens to reproof gets understanding.

Proverbs 16:17
The highway of the upright is to depart from evil. He who keeps his way preserves his soul.

Proverbs 19:8
He who gets wisdom loves his own soul. He who keeps understanding shall find good.

Proverbs 19:16
He who keeps the commandment keeps his soul, but he who is contemptuous in his ways shall die.

Proverbs 21:23
Whoever guards his mouth and his tongue keeps his soul from troubles.

* * *

Isaiah

Isaiah 58:10, 11
...and if you pour out your soul to the hungry, and satisfy the afflicted soul, then your light will rise in darkness, and

your obscurity will be as the noonday; and Yahweh will guide you continually, satisfy your soul in dry places, and make your bones strong. You will be like a watered garden, and like a spring of water whose waters don't fail.

Isaiah 61:10

I will greatly rejoice in Yahweh! My soul will be joyful in my God, for he has clothed me with the garments of salvation. He has covered me with the robe of righteousness, as a bridegroom decks himself with a garland and as a bride adorns herself with her jewels.

* * *

Jeremiah

Jeremiah 6:16

Yahweh says, "Stand in the ways and see, and ask for the old paths, 'Where is the good way?' and walk in it, and you will find rest for your souls.

Jeremiah 20:13

Sing to Yahweh! Praise Yahweh, for he has delivered the soul of the needy from the hand of evildoers.

Jeremiah 31:14

I will satiate the soul of the priests with fatness, and my people will be satisfied with my goodness," says Yahweh.

Jeremiah 31:25

For I have satiated the weary soul, and I have replenished every sorrowful soul.

* * *

Lamentations

Lamentations 3:24
"Yahweh is my portion," says my soul. "Therefore I will hope in him."

Lamentations 3:25
Yahweh is good to those who wait for him, to the soul who seeks him.

Lamentations 3:58
Lord, you have pleaded the causes of my soul. You have redeemed my life.

* * *

Ezekiel

Ezekiel 18:4
Behold, all souls are mine; as the soul of the father, so also the soul of the son is mine. The soul who sins, he shall die.

Ezekiel 18:27
Again, when the wicked man turns away from his wickedness

that he has committed, and does that which is lawful and right, he will save his soul alive.

* * *

New Testament

Matthew

Matthew 10:28

Don't be afraid of those who kill the body, but are not able to kill the soul. Rather, fear him who is able to destroy both soul and body in Gehenna.

Matthew 11:29

Take my yoke upon you and learn from me, for I am gentle and humble in heart; and you will find rest for your souls.

Matthew 22:37

Jesus said to him, "'You shall love the Lord your God with all your heart, with all your soul, and with all your mind.'"

* * *

Mark

Mark 12:29-31

Jesus answered, "The greatest is, 'Hear, Israel, the Lord our God, the Lord is one: you shall love the Lord your God with all

your heart, and with all your soul, and with all your mind, and with all your strength.' This is the first commandment. The second is like this, 'You shall love your neighbour as yourself.' There is no other commandment greater than these."

* * *

Luke

Luke 10:27

He answered, "You shall love the Lord your God with all your heart, with all your soul, with all your strength, and with all your mind; and your neighbour as yourself."

* * *

Acts

Acts 4:32

The multitude of those who believed were of one heart and soul. Not one of them claimed that anything of the things which he possessed was his own, but they had all things in common.

* * *

Romans

Romans 13:1

Let every soul be in subjection to the higher authorities, for there is no authority except from God, and those who exist are ordained by God.

* * *

1 Corinthians

1 Corinthians 15:45

So also it is written, "The first man, Adam, became a living soul." The last Adam became a life-giving spirit.

* * *

Philippians

Philippians 1:27, 28

Only let your way of life be worthy of the Good News of Christ, that whether I come and see you or am absent, I may hear of your state, that you stand firm in one spirit, with one soul striving for the faith of the Good News; and in nothing frightened by the adversaries, which is for them a proof of destruction, but to you of salvation, and that from God.

* * *

1 Thessalonians

1 Thessalonians 5:23

May the God of peace himself sanctify you completely. May your whole spirit, soul, and body be preserved blameless at the coming of our Lord Jesus Christ.

* * *

Hebrews

Hebrews 4:12

For the word of God is living and active, and sharper than any two-edged sword, piercing even to the dividing of soul and spirit, of both joints and marrow, and is able to discern the thoughts and intentions of the heart.

Hebrews 6:19, 20

This hope we have as an anchor of the soul, a hope both sure and steadfast and entering into that which is within the veil; where as a forerunner Jesus entered for us, having become a high priest forever after the order of Melchizedek.

Hebrews 10:39

But we are not of those who shrink back to destruction, but of those who have faith to the saving of the soul.

Hebrews 13:17

Obey your leaders and submit to them, for they watch on behalf of your souls, as those who will give account, that they may do this with joy, and not with groaning, for that would be unprofitable for you.

* * *

James

James 1:21

Therefore, putting away all filthiness and overflowing of wickedness, receive with humility the implanted word, which is able to save your souls.

James 5:19, 20

Brothers, if any among you wanders from the truth and someone turns him back, let him know that he who turns a sinner from the error of his way will save a soul from death and will cover a multitude of sins.

* * *

1 Peter

1 Peter 1:8, 9

In him, though now you don't see him, yet believing, you rejoice greatly with joy that is unspeakable and full of glory, receiving the result of your faith, the salvation of your souls.

1 Peter 1:22, 23

Seeing you have purified your souls in your obedience to the truth through the Spirit in sincere brotherly affection, love one another from the heart fervently, having been born again, not of corruptible seed, but of incorruptible, through the word of God, which lives and remains forever.

1 Peter 2:11

Beloved, I beg you as foreigners and pilgrims, to abstain from fleshly lusts, which war against the soul

1 Peter 2:25

For you were going astray like sheep; but now you have returned to the Shepherd and Overseer of your souls.

1 Peter 4:19

Therefore let them also who suffer according to the will of God in doing good entrust their souls to him, as to a faithful Creator.

* * *

3 John

3 John 1:2

Beloved, I pray that you may prosper in all things and be healthy, even as your soul prospers.

8

All Your Mind

The mind encompasses many aspects for us, including our intellect, thoughts, emotions, desires, and conscience. The following selection of verses will explore each of these facets and how we need to keep our minds in check and focused on God and His commandments to avoid falling into sin. One of our main goals is to achieve what Paul wrote in his epistle to the Romans: to be "transformed by the renewing of your mind". Including the mind in the Greatest Commandment underscores the importance of intellectual engagement in our faith journey. We are not expected to leave our brains at the door when we come to faith in God.

Loving God with our mind involves actively seeking to know Him through study and reflection, allowing our thoughts to be shaped by Scriptural truths. It calls for discernment and wisdom in our daily decisions, integrating faith with reason. This holistic approach ensures that our worship is not merely emotional but deeply rooted in a well-reasoned understanding of God's character and will, safeguarding against false teachings and fostering a robust, sincere relationship with Him.

Early church writers highlighted how the Word of God is the very reason, wisdom, and mind of God, since the underlying Greek word λόγος (logos), often translated as "Word", has a much wider meaning than typically conveyed in English. Justin Martyr, in his *First Apology*, wrote, *"Reason (or the Word, the Logos) Himself, who took shape, and became man, and was called Jesus Christ."*.

Read through these verses, but don't *just* read—pray at the same time and let the Holy Spirit guide you as you read through these verses of Scripture so that you may be led to the passages that speak to you most, helping you conform your mind more to Christ and His will for you.

* * *

Old Testament

Psalms

Psalm 7:9
Oh let the wickedness of the wicked come to an end, but establish the righteous; their minds and hearts are searched by the righteous God.

Psalm 10:4
The wicked, in the pride of his face, has no room in his thoughts for God.

Psalm 26:2

Examine me, Yahweh, and prove me. Try my heart and my mind.

Psalm 94:11
Yahweh knows the thoughts of man, that they are futile.

Psalm 94:19
In the multitude of my thoughts within me, your comforts delight my soul.

Psalm 119:113
I hate double-minded men, but I love your law.

Psalm 139:2, 23
You know my sitting down and my rising up. You perceive my thoughts from afar. ... Search me, God, and know my heart. Try me, and know my thoughts.

* * *

Proverbs

Proverbs 12:5, 8
The thoughts of the righteous are just, but the advice of the wicked is deceitful. ... A man shall be commended according to his wisdom, but he who has a warped mind shall be despised.

Proverbs 15:26
Yahweh detests the thoughts of the wicked, but the thoughts

of the pure are pleasing.

* * *

Ecclesiastes

Ecclesiastes 10:20

Don't curse the king, no, not in your thoughts; and don't curse the rich in your bedroom: for a bird of the sky may carry your voice, and that which has wings may tell the matter.

* * *

Isaiah

Isaiah 26:3

You will keep whoever's mind is steadfast in perfect peace, because he trusts in you.

Isaiah 55:7

Let the wicked forsake his way, and the unrighteous man his thoughts. Let him return to Yahweh, and he will have mercy on him, to our God, for he will freely pardon.

* * *

Jeremiah

Jeremiah 17:10

"I, Yahweh, search the mind. I try the heart, even to give every man according to his ways, according to the fruit of his doings."

* * *

Lamentations

Lamentations 3:21, 22

This I recall to my mind; therefore I have hope. It is because of Yahweh's loving kindnesses that we are not consumed, because his compassion doesn't fail.

* * *

New Testament

Matthew 15:19

For out of the heart come evil thoughts, murders, adulteries, sexual sins, thefts, false testimony, and blasphemies.

Matthew 16:23

But he turned and said to Peter, "Get behind me, Satan! You are a stumbling block to me, for you are not setting your mind on the things of God, but on the things of men."

Matthew 22:37
Jesus said to him, "'You shall love the Lord your God with all your heart, with all your soul, and with all your mind.'"

* * *

Mark

Mark 7:21, 22
For from within, out of the hearts of men, proceed evil thoughts, adulteries, sexual sins, murders, thefts, covetings, wickedness, deceit, lustful desires, an evil eye, blasphemy, pride, and foolishness.

Mark 8:33
But he, turning around, and seeing his disciples, rebuked Peter, and said, "Get behind me, Satan! For you have in mind not the things of God, but the things of men."

Mark 12:30
...you shall love the Lord your God with all your heart, and with all your soul, and with all your mind, and with all your strength.' This is the first commandment.

* * *

Luke

Luke 10:27
He answered, "You shall love the Lord your God with all your heart, with all your soul, with all your strength, and with all your mind; and your neighbour as yourself."

Luke 24:45, 46
Then he opened their minds, that they might understand the Scriptures. He said to them, "Thus it is written, and thus it was necessary for the Christ to suffer and to rise from the dead the third day..."

* * *

Acts

Acts 17:11
Now these were more noble than those in Thessalonica, in that they received the word with all readiness of mind, examining the Scriptures daily to see whether these things were so.

Acts 24:16
In this I also practice always having a conscience void of offence toward God and men.

* * *

Romans

Romans 2:14-16

(for when Gentiles who don't have the law do by nature the things of the law, these, not having the law, are a law to themselves, in that they show the work of the law written in their hearts, their conscience testifying with them, and their thoughts among themselves accusing or else excusing them) in the day when God will judge the secrets of men, according to my Good News, by Jesus Christ.

Romans 7:22, 23

For I delight in God's law after the inward person, but I see a different law in my members, warring against the law of my mind, and bringing me into captivity under the law of sin which is in my members.

Romans 7:25

I thank God through Jesus Christ, our Lord! So then with the mind, I myself serve God's law, but with the flesh, sin's law.

Romans 8:5-7

For those who live according to the flesh set their minds on the things of the flesh, but those who live according to the Spirit, the things of the Spirit. For the mind of the flesh is death, but the mind of the Spirit is life and peace; because the mind of the flesh is hostile toward God; for it is not subject to God's law, neither indeed can it be.

Romans 12:2

Don't be conformed to this world, but be transformed by the

renewing of your mind, so that you may prove what is the good, well-pleasing, and perfect will of God.

Romans 12:16

Be of the same mind one toward another. Don't set your mind on high things, but associate with the humble. Don't be wise in your own conceits.

Romans 15:5, 6

Now the God of perseverance and of encouragement grant you to be of the same mind with one another according to Christ Jesus, that with one accord you may with one mouth glorify the God and Father of our Lord Jesus Christ.

* * *

1 Corinthians

1 Corinthians 1:10

Now I beg you, brothers, through the name of our Lord, Jesus Christ, that you all speak the same thing, and that there be no divisions among you, but that you be perfected together in the same mind and in the same judgment.

1 Corinthians 2:16

"For who has known the mind of the Lord, that he should instruct him?" But we have Christ's mind.

1 Corinthians 8:6-12

...yet to us there is one God, the Father, of whom are all things, and we for him; and one Lord, Jesus Christ, through whom are all things, and we live through him. However, that knowledge isn't in all men. But some, with consciousness of the idol until now, eat as of a thing sacrificed to an idol, and their conscience, being weak, is defiled. But food will not commend us to God. For neither, if we don't eat, are we the worse; nor, if we eat, are we the better. But be careful that by no means does this liberty of yours become a stumbling block to the weak. For if a man sees you who have knowledge sitting in an idol's temple, won't his conscience, if he is weak, be emboldened to eat things sacrificed to idols? And through your knowledge, he who is weak perishes, the brother for whose sake Christ died. Thus, sinning against the brothers, and wounding their conscience when it is weak, you sin against Christ.

1 Corinthians 10:25-27

Whatever is sold in the butcher shop, eat, asking no question for the sake of conscience, for "the earth is the Lord's, and its fullness." But if one of those who don't believe invites you to a meal, and you are inclined to go, eat whatever is set before you, asking no questions for the sake of conscience.

1 Corinthians 14:20

Brothers, don't be children in thoughts, yet in malice be babies, but in thoughts be mature.

* * *

2 Corinthians

2 Corinthians 1:12

For our boasting is this: the testimony of our conscience, that in holiness and sincerity of God, not in fleshly wisdom but in the grace of God we behaved ourselves in the world, and more abundantly toward you.

2 Corinthians 5:11

Knowing therefore the fear of the Lord, we persuade men, but we are revealed to God, and I hope that we are revealed also in your consciences.

2 Corinthians 11:3

But I am afraid that somehow, as the serpent deceived Eve in his craftiness, so your minds might be corrupted from the simplicity that is in Christ.

2 Corinthians 13:11

Finally, brothers, rejoice! Be perfected. Be comforted. Be of the same mind. Live in peace, and the God of love and peace will be with you.

* * *

1 Timothy

1 Timothy 1:5

...but the goal of this command is love, out of a pure heart and a good conscience and sincere faith...

1 Timothy 1:19

...holding faith and a good conscience, which some having thrust away made a shipwreck concerning the faith...

1 Timothy 3:9

...holding the mystery of the faith in a pure conscience.

* * *

Ephesians

Ephesians 4:17, 18

This I say therefore, and testify in the Lord, that you no longer walk as the rest of the Gentiles also walk, in the futility of their mind, being darkened in their understanding, alienated from the life of God because of the ignorance that is in them, because of the hardening of their hearts.

Ephesians 4:23, 24

...and that you be renewed in the spirit of your mind, and put on the new man, who in the likeness of God has been created in righteousness and holiness of truth.

* * *

Philippians

Philippians 2:5-7
Have this in your mind, which was also in Christ Jesus, who, existing in the form of God, didn't consider equality with God a thing to be grasped, but emptied himself, taking the form of a servant, being made in the likeness of men.

Philippians 3:16
Nevertheless, to the extent that we have already attained, let's walk by the same rule. Let's be of the same mind.

Philippians 4:7
And the peace of God, which surpasses all understanding, will guard your hearts and your thoughts in Christ Jesus.

* * *

Colossians

Colossians 1:21, 22
You, being in past times alienated and enemies in your mind in your evil deeds, yet now he has reconciled in the body of his flesh through death, to present you holy and without defect and blameless before him...

Colossians 3:2
Set your mind on the things that are above, not on the things that are on the earth.

* * *

Titus

Titus 1:8

...but given to hospitality, a lover of good, sober minded, fair, holy, self-controlled...

Titus 1:15

To the pure, all things are pure; but to those who are defiled and unbelieving, nothing is pure; but both their mind and their conscience are defiled.

Titus 2:1-6

But say the things which fit sound doctrine, that older men should be temperate, sensible, sober minded, sound in faith, in love, and in perseverance: and that older women likewise be reverent in behaviour, not slanderers nor enslaved to much wine, teachers of that which is good, that they may train the young wives to love their husbands, to love their children, to be sober minded, chaste, workers at home, kind, being in subjection to their own husbands, that God's word may not be blasphemed. Likewise, exhort the younger men to be sober minded.

* * *

Hebrews

Hebrews 4:12

For the word of God is living and active, and sharper than any two-edged sword, piercing even to the dividing of soul and spirit, of both joints and marrow, and is able to discern the thoughts and intentions of the heart.

Hebrews 8:10

"For this is the covenant that I will make with the house of Israel. After those days," says the Lord; "I will put my laws into their mind, I will also write them on their heart. I will be their God, and they will be my people."

Hebrews 9:13-14

For if the blood of goats and bulls, and the ashes of a heifer sprinkling those who have been defiled, sanctify to the cleanness of the flesh, how much more will the blood of Christ, who through the eternal Spirit offered himself without defect to God, cleanse your conscience from dead works to serve the living God?

Hebrews 10:16

"This is the covenant that I will make with them: 'After those days,' says the Lord, 'I will put my laws on their heart, I will also write them on their mind;'"

Hebrews 10:22-23

...let's draw near with a true heart in fullness of faith, having our hearts sprinkled from an evil conscience, and having our body washed with pure water, let's hold fast the confession of our hope without wavering; for he who promised is faithful.

* * *

James

James 1:6-8

But let him ask in faith, without any doubting, for he who doubts is like a wave of the sea, driven by the wind and tossed. For that man shouldn't think that he will receive anything from the Lord. He is a double-minded man, unstable in all his ways.

James 2:3, 4

...and you pay special attention to him who wears the fine clothing and say, "Sit here in a good place;" and you tell the poor man, "Stand there," or "Sit by my footstool" haven't you shown partiality among yourselves, and become judges with evil thoughts?

James 4:8

Draw near to God, and he will draw near to you. Cleanse your hands, you sinners. Purify your hearts, you double-minded.

* * *

1 Peter

1 Peter 1:13

Therefore prepare your minds for action. Be sober, and set your hope fully on the grace that will be brought to you at the revelation of Jesus Christ

1 Peter 2:19

For it is commendable if someone endures pain, suffering unjustly, because of conscience toward God.

1 Peter 3:8

Finally, all of you be like-minded, compassionate, loving as brothers, tenderhearted, courteous, not rendering evil for evil, or insult for insult; but instead blessing, knowing that you were called to this, that you may inherit a blessing.

1 Peter 3:15, 16

But sanctify the Lord God in your hearts. Always be ready to give an answer to everyone who asks you a reason concerning the hope that is in you, with humility and fear, having a good conscience. Thus, while you are spoken against as evildoers, they may be disappointed who curse your good way of life in Christ.

1 Peter 3:21

This is a symbol of baptism, which now saves you—not the putting away of the filth of the flesh, but the answer of a good conscience toward God, through the resurrection of Jesus Christ, who is at the right hand of God, having gone into heaven, angels and authorities and powers being made subject to him.

1 Peter 4:1, 2

Therefore, since Christ suffered for us in the flesh, arm yourselves also with the same mind; for he who has suffered in the flesh has ceased from sin, that you no longer should live the rest of your time in the flesh for the lusts of men, but for the will of God.

1 Peter 4:7

But the end of all things is near. Therefore be of sound mind, self-controlled, and sober in prayer.

9

All Your Strength

Loving and serving God with all our strength highlights a commitment that involves every aspect of our being. The "strength" aspect is explicitly mentioned in Mark's Gospel (12:30), reflecting the wording of Deuteronomy 6:5. In contrast, Matthew's account doesn't mention strength and seems to reference Deuteronomy 10:12, which focuses on the heart and soul, alongside obedience.

With this in mind, the need for our strength is multifaceted. It encompasses physical devotion and obedience, seen in our actions and perseverance in following and trusting in God; emotional resilience, vital for overcoming challenges and maintaining our joy and peace; and mental and moral fortitude, necessary for disciplined thoughts and moral integrity. Loving God with all our strength means fully committing our physical, emotional, mental, and moral energies to Him, ensuring our entire being is engaged in following this commandment throughout our lives.

Read through these verses, but don't *just* read—pray at the same time and let the Holy Spirit guide you as you reflect on these verses of Scripture, leading you to the passages that resonate deeply with you. May this help you to love and follow God with all *your* strength, aligning every aspect of your life and being with His will.

* * *

Old Testament

Exodus

Exodus 15:2

   Yah is my strength and song. He has become my salvation. This is my God, and I will praise him; my father's God, and I will exalt him.

* * *

1 Chronicles

1 Chronicles 16:11

   Seek Yahweh and his strength. Seek his face forever more.

1 Chronicles 29:12

   Both riches and honour come from you, and you rule over all! In your hand is power and might! It is in your hand to make great, and to give strength to all!

* * *

Psalms

Psalm 18:1
I love you, Yahweh, my strength.

Psalm 18:31, 32
For who is God, except Yahweh? Who is a rock, besides our God, the God who arms me with strength, and makes my way perfect?

Psalm 18:39
For you have armed me with strength to the battle. You have subdued under me those who rose up against me.

Psalm 27:1
Yahweh is my light and my salvation. Whom shall I fear? Yahweh is the strength of my life. Of whom shall I be afraid?

Psalm 28:7, 8
Yahweh is my strength and my shield. My heart has trusted in him, and I am helped. Therefore my heart greatly rejoices. With my song I will thank him. Yahweh is their strength. He is a stronghold of salvation to his anointed.

Psalm 29:11
Yahweh will give strength to his people. Yahweh will bless his people with peace.

Psalm 43:2

For you are the God of my strength. Why have you rejected me? Why do I go mourning because of the oppression of the enemy?

Psalm 46:1

God is our refuge and strength, a very present help in trouble.

Psalm 59:9

Oh, my Strength, I watch for you, for God is my high tower.

Psalm 59:16

But I will sing of your strength. Yes, I will sing aloud of your loving kindness in the morning. For you have been my high tower, a refuge in the day of my distress.

Psalm 59:17

To you, my strength, I will sing praises. For God is my high tower, the God of my mercy.

Psalm 62:7

My salvation and my honour is with God. The rock of my strength, and my refuge, is in God.

Psalm 68:28

Your God has commanded your strength. Strengthen, God, that which you have done for us.

Psalm 68:35

You are awesome, God, in your sanctuaries. The God of Israel gives strength and power to his people. Praise be to God!

Psalm 73:26

My flesh and my heart fails, but God is the strength of my heart and my portion forever.

Psalm 81:1

Sing aloud to God, our strength! Make a joyful shout to the God of Jacob!

Psalm 84:5

Blessed are those whose strength is in you, who have set their hearts on a pilgrimage.

Psalm 86:16

Turn to me, and have mercy on me! Give your strength to your servant. Save the son of your servant.

Psalm 89:15-17

Blessed are the people who learn to acclaim you. They walk in the light of your presence, Yahweh. In your name they rejoice all day. In your righteousness, they are exalted. For you are the glory of their strength. In your favour, our horn will be exalted.

Psalm 105:4

Seek Yahweh and his strength. Seek his face forever more.

Psalm 118:14

Yah is my strength and song. He has become my salvation.

Psalm 119:28

My soul is weary with sorrow: strengthen me according to your word.

Psalm 138:3

In the day that I called, you answered me. You encouraged me with strength in my soul.

Psalm 140:7

Yahweh, the Lord, the strength of my salvation, you have covered my head in the day of battle.

Psalm 147:13

For he has strengthened the bars of your gates. He has blessed your children within you.

* * *

Proverbs

Proverbs 20:29

The glory of young men is their strength. The splendour of old men is their gray hair.

* * *

Ecclesiastes

Ecclesiastes 7:19

Wisdom is a strength to the wise man more than ten rulers who are in a city.

* * *

Isaiah

Isaiah 12:2

Behold, God is my salvation. I will trust, and will not be afraid; for Yah, Yahweh, is my strength and song; and he has become my salvation.

Isaiah 17:10

For you have forgotten the God of your salvation, and have not remembered the rock of your strength. Therefore you plant pleasant plants, and set out foreign seedlings.

Isaiah 33:2

Yahweh, be gracious to us. We have waited for you. Be our strength every morning, our salvation also in the time of trouble.

Isaiah 35:3, 4

Strengthen the weak hands, and make the feeble knees firm. Tell those who have a fearful heart, "Be strong! Don't be afraid! Behold, your God will come with vengeance, God's retribution. He will come and save you.

Isaiah 40:29-31

He gives power to the weak. He increases the strength of him who has no might. Even the youths faint and get weary, and the young men utterly fall; but those who wait for Yahweh will renew their strength. They will mount up with wings like eagles.

They will run, and not be weary. They will walk, and not faint.

Isaiah 41:10
Don't you be afraid, for I am with you. Don't be dismayed, for I am your God. I will strengthen you. Yes, I will help you. Yes, I will uphold you with the right hand of my righteousness.

Isaiah 45:5, 6
I am Yahweh, and there is no one else. Besides me, there is no God. I will strengthen you, though you have not known me, that they may know from the rising of the sun, and from the west, that there is no one besides me. I am Yahweh, and there is no one else.

Isaiah 49:5
...for I am honourable in Yahweh's eyes, and my God has become my strength.

* * *

Jeremiah

Jeremiah 15:11
Yahweh said, "Most certainly I will strengthen you for good. Most certainly I will cause the enemy to make supplication to you in the time of evil and in the time of affliction.

Jeremiah 16:19
Yahweh, my strength, and my stronghold, and my refuge in the day of affliction, the nations will come to you from the ends

of the earth, and will say, "Our fathers have inherited nothing but lies, vanity and things in which there is no profit.

* * *

Lamentations

Lamentations 3:18
I said, "My strength has perished, along with my expectation from Yahweh."

* * *

Habakkuk

Habakkuk 3:19
Yahweh, the Lord, is my strength. He makes my feet like deer's feet, and enables me to go in high places.

* * *

New Testament

Mark

Mark 12:30
you shall love the Lord your God with all your heart, and with all your soul, and with all your mind, and with all your

strength.' This is the first commandment.

* * *

Luke

Luke 10:27
He answered, "You shall love the Lord your God with all your heart, with all your soul, with all your strength, and with all your mind; and your neighbour as yourself."

* * *

Ephesians

Ephesians 3:14-19
For this cause, I bow my knees to the Father of our Lord Jesus Christ, from whom every family in heaven and on earth is named, that he would grant you, according to the riches of his glory, that you may be strengthened with power through his Spirit in the inner person, that Christ may dwell in your hearts through faith, to the end that you, being rooted and grounded in love, may be strengthened to comprehend with all the saints what is the width and length and height and depth, and to know Christ's love which surpasses knowledge, that you may be filled with all the fullness of God.

Ephesians 6:10
Finally, be strong in the Lord, and in the strength of his might.

* * *

Philippians

Philippians 4:13
I can do all things through Christ, who strengthens me.

* * *

Colossians

Colossians 1:9-14
For this cause, we also, since the day we heard this, don't cease praying and making requests for you, that you may be filled with the knowledge of his will in all spiritual wisdom and understanding, that you may walk worthily of the Lord, to please him in all respects, bearing fruit in every good work and increasing in the knowledge of God, strengthened with all power, according to the might of his glory, for all endurance and perseverance with joy, giving thanks to the Father, who made us fit to be partakers of the inheritance of the saints in light, who delivered us out of the power of darkness, and translated us into the Kingdom of the Son of his love, in whom we have our redemption, the forgiveness of our sins.

* * *

2 Timothy

2 Timothy 2:1

You therefore, my child, be strengthened in the grace that is in Christ Jesus.

* * *

1 Peter

1 Peter 4:11

If anyone speaks, let it be as it were the very words of God. If anyone serves, let it be as of the strength which God supplies, that in all things God may be glorified through Jesus Christ, to whom belong the glory and the dominion forever and ever. Amen.

1 Peter 5:10

But may the God of all grace, who called you to his eternal glory by Christ Jesus, after you have suffered a little while, perfect, establish, strengthen, and settle you.

10

Love Your Neighbour as Yourself

In light of the Greatest Commandment the call to love our neighbours follows naturally from our love for God. Loving our neighbours involves a holistic approach, encompassing acts of kindness, empathy, and respect. It is about meeting both their physical, spiritual, and emotional needs, promoting justice and peace, and sharing in their joys and sorrows.

The Ten Commandments, often seen as primarily God-focused (or sometimes as a list of *thou shalt nots*) are equally as people-focused. While the first four commandments emphasise our relationship with God, such as having no other gods and keeping the Sabbath holy, the last six direct us to love and respect others. These commandments instruct us to honour our parents, avoid murder, adultery, theft, false testimony, and coveting what belongs to others (Exodus 20:12-17). To love our neighbours means practising forgiveness, offering support, and being hospitable. It involves living with integrity, showing generosity, and encouraging their spiritual growth. This comprehensive approach reflects the deep love that God has for each of us and fulfils the commandment to love others as ourselves. Through our actions and attitudes, we can create a compassionate and just community, mirroring the love of God in every aspect of life.

Read through these verses, but don't *just* read—pray at the same time and let the Holy Spirit guide you as you reflect on these verses of Scripture, leading you to the passages that resonate deeply with you. May this help you to love your neighbour as yourself and live out the kind of love that God wants from us towards others made in his image.

* * *

Old Testament

Exodus

Exodus 20:16, 17

"You shall not give false testimony against your neighbour. You shall not covet your neighbour's house. You shall not covet your neighbour's wife, nor his male servant, nor his female servant, nor his ox, nor his donkey, nor anything that is your neighbour's."

* * *

Leviticus

Leviticus 19:15-18

"You shall do no injustice in judgment. You shall not be partial to the poor, nor show favouritism to the great; but you shall judge your neighbour in righteousness. You shall not go around as a slanderer among your people. 'You shall not endanger the life of your neighbour. I am Yahweh. You shall not hate your brother in your heart. You shall surely rebuke your neighbour, and not bear sin because of him. You shall not take vengeance, nor bear any grudge against the children of your people; but you shall love your neighbour as yourself. I am Yahweh."

Leviticus 25:14

If you sell anything to your neighbour, or buy from your neighbour, you shall not wrong one another.

* * *

Deuteronomy

Deuteronomy 5:20

"You shall not give false testimony against your neighbour."

Deuteronomy 15:2

This is the way it shall be done: every creditor shall release that which he has lent to his neighbour. He shall not require payment from his neighbour and his brother, because Yahweh's release has been proclaimed.

* * *

Proverbs

Proverbs 3:29

Don't devise evil against your neighbour, since he dwells securely by you.

Proverbs 11:9

With his mouth the godless man destroys his neighbour, but the righteous will be delivered through knowledge.

Proverbs 11:12

One who despises his neighbour is void of wisdom, but a man of understanding holds his peace.

Proverbs 14:21

He who despises his neighbour sins, but he who has pity on the poor is blessed.

Proverbs 24:28

Don't be a witness against your neighbour without cause. Don't deceive with your lips.

Proverbs 25:17

Let your foot be seldom in your neighbour's house, lest he be weary of you, and hate you.

Proverbs 27:14

He who blesses his neighbour with a loud voice early in the

morning, it will be taken as a curse by him.

* * *

Isaiah

Isaiah 41:6
Everyone helps his neighbour. They say to their brothers, "Be strong!"

* * *

Jeremiah

Jeremiah 7:5-7
For if you thoroughly amend your ways and your doings, if you thoroughly execute justice between a man and his neighbour; if you don't oppress the foreigner, the fatherless, and the widow, and don't shed innocent blood in this place, and don't walk after other gods to your own hurt; then I will cause you to dwell in this place, in the land that I gave to your fathers, from of old even forever more.

Jeremiah 34:15
You had now turned, and had done that which is right in my eyes, in every man proclaiming liberty to his neighbour.

* * *

Zechariah

Zechariah 8:16-18

These are the things that you shall do: speak every man the truth with his neighbour. Execute the judgment of truth and peace in your gates, and let none of you devise evil in your hearts against his neighbour, and love no false oath: for all these are things that I hate," says Yahweh.

* * *

New Testament

Matthew

Matthew 5:43-45

"You have heard that it was said, 'You shall love your neighbour and hate your enemy.' But I tell you, love your enemies, bless those who curse you, do good to those who hate you, and pray for those who mistreat you and persecute you, that you may be children of your Father who is in heaven. For he makes his sun to rise on the evil and the good, and sends rain on the just and the unjust.

Matthew 19:19

'Honour your father and your mother.' And, 'You shall love your neighbour as yourself.'"

Matthew 22:37-40

Jesus said to him, "'You shall love the Lord your God with

all your heart, with all your soul, and with all your mind.' This is the first and great commandment. A second likewise is this, 'You shall love your neighbour as yourself.' The whole law and the prophets depend on these two commandments."

* * *

Mark

Mark 12:29–31

Jesus answered, "The greatest is, 'Hear, Israel, the Lord our God, the Lord is one: you shall love the Lord your God with all your heart, and with all your soul, and with all your mind, and with all your strength.' This is the first commandment. The second is like this, 'You shall love your neighbour as yourself.' There is no other commandment greater than these."

* * *

Luke

Luke 10:26–28

He said to him, "What is written in the law? How do you read it?" He answered, "You shall love the Lord your God with all your heart, with all your soul, with all your strength, and with all your mind; and your neighbour as yourself." He said to him, "You have answered correctly. Do this, and you will live."

Luke 14:12-14

He also said to the one who had invited him, "When you make a dinner or a supper, don't call your friends, nor your brothers, nor your kinsmen, nor rich neighbours, or perhaps they might also return the favour, and pay you back. But when you make a feast, ask the poor, the maimed, the lame, or the blind; and you will be blessed, because they don't have the resources to repay you. For you will be repaid in the resurrection of the righteous."

* * *

John

John 13:34, 35

A new commandment I give to you, that you love one another. Just as I have loved you, you also love one another. By this everyone will know that you are my disciples, if you have love for one another.

John 15:12-14

"This is my commandment, that you love one another, even as I have loved you. Greater love has no one than this, that someone lay down his life for his friends. You are my friends, if you do whatever I command you.

John 15:17-19

I command these things to you, that you may love one another. If the world hates you, you know that it has hated me before it hated you. If you were of the world, the world would love its own. But because you are not of the world, since I chose you out of the world, therefore the world hates you.

* * *

Romans

Romans 12:9-13

Let love be without hypocrisy. Abhor that which is evil. Cling to that which is good. In love of the brothers be tenderly affectionate to one another; in honour preferring one another; 11 not lagging in diligence; fervent in spirit; serving the Lord; rejoicing in hope; enduring in troubles; continuing steadfastly in prayer; contributing to the needs of the saints; given to hospitality.

Romans 13:8-10

Owe no one anything, except to love one another; for he who loves his neighbour has fulfilled the law. For the commandments, "You shall not commit adultery," "You shall not murder," "You shall not steal," "You shall not covet," and whatever other commandments there are, are all summed up in this saying, namely, "You shall love your neighbour as yourself." Love doesn't harm a neighbour. Love therefore is the fulfilment of the law.

Romans 15:2

Let each one of us please his neighbour for that which is good, to be building him up.

* * *

1 Corinthians

1 Corinthians 6:1-3

Dare any of you, having a matter against his neighbour, go to law before the unrighteous, and not before the saints? Don't you know that the saints will judge the world? And if the world is judged by you, are you unworthy to judge the smallest matters? Don't you know that we will judge angels? How much more, things that pertain to this life?

1 Corinthians 10:24

Let no one seek his own, but each one his neighbour's good.

* * *

Galatians

Galatians 5:13-15

For you, brothers, were called for freedom. Only don't use your freedom for gain to the flesh, but through love be servants to one another. For the whole law is fulfilled in one word, in this: "You shall love your neighbour as yourself." But if you bite and devour one another, be careful that you don't consume one another.

* * *

Ephesians

Ephesians 4:1-3

I therefore, the prisoner in the Lord, beg you to walk worthily of the calling with which you were called, with all lowliness and humility, with patience, bearing with one another in love, being eager to keep the unity of the Spirit in the bond of peace.

Ephesians 4:25-27

Therefore putting away falsehood, speak truth each one with his neighbour. For we are members of one another. "Be angry, and don't sin." Don't let the sun go down on your wrath, and don't give place to the devil.

* * *

1 Thessalonians

1 Thessalonians 3:12, 13

May the Lord make you to increase and abound in love toward one another, and toward all men, even as we also do toward you, to the end he may establish your hearts blameless in holiness before our God and Father at the coming of our Lord Jesus with all his saints.

1 Thessalonians 4:9

But concerning brotherly love, you have no need that one write to you. For you yourselves are taught by God to love one another

* * *

2 Thessalonians

2 Thessalonians 1:3

We are bound to always give thanks to God for you, brothers, even as it is appropriate, because your faith grows exceedingly, and the love of each and every one of you toward one another abounds...

* * *

Hebrews

Hebrews 10:24

Let's consider how to provoke one another to love and good works, not forsaking our own assembling together, as the custom of some is, but exhorting one another, and so much the more as you see the Day approaching.

* * *

James

James 2:7-9

Don't they blaspheme the honourable name by which you are called? However, if you fulfil the royal law according to the Scripture, "You shall love your neighbour as yourself," you do well. But if you show partiality, you commit sin, being convicted by the law as transgressors.

* * *

1 Peter

1 Peter 1:22

Seeing you have purified your souls in your obedience to the truth through the Spirit in sincere brotherly affection, love one another from the heart fervently, having been born again, not of corruptible seed, but of incorruptible, through the word of God, which lives and remains forever.

1 Peter 5:14

Greet one another with a kiss of love. Peace be to all of you who are in Christ Jesus. Amen.

* * *

1 John

1 John 3:11

For this is the message which you heard from the beginning, that we should love one another...

1 John 3:23

This is his commandment, that we should believe in the

name of his Son, Jesus Christ, and love one another, even as he commanded.

1 John 4:7

Beloved, let's love one another, for love is of God; and everyone who loves has been born of God, and knows God.

1 John 4:11

Beloved, if God loved us in this way, we also ought to love one another.

1 John 4:12

No one has seen God at any time. If we love one another, God remains in us, and his love has been perfected in us.

2 John 1:5, 6

Now I beg you, dear lady, not as though I wrote to you a new commandment, but that which we had from the beginning, that we love one another. This is love, that we should walk according to his commandments. This is the commandment, even as you heard from the beginning, that you should walk in it.

III

Resources

The following pages will give you some liturgical prayers and resources to help you with your walk with God, which you can use at any time or as part of the Lectio Divina method.
I will include some options from various traditions, such as: Anglican, Roman Catholic, and Eastern Orthodox.

11

Spiritual Aids

Throughout Christian history, various aids have been developed to help us focus our minds better as we pray, and avoid getting distracted so easily.

The three I will mention here are: the Rosary, Anglican prayer beads, and Orthodox prayer ropes. The Rosary and Anglican Prayer Beads look very similar, except that in the Rosary there are 10 smaller beads in each section (or "decade"), and on the Anglican one there are only 7 beads (called "weeks").

Use the prayers in the next chapter in combination with these spiritual prayer aids as a way to enhance and focus your prayer-life.

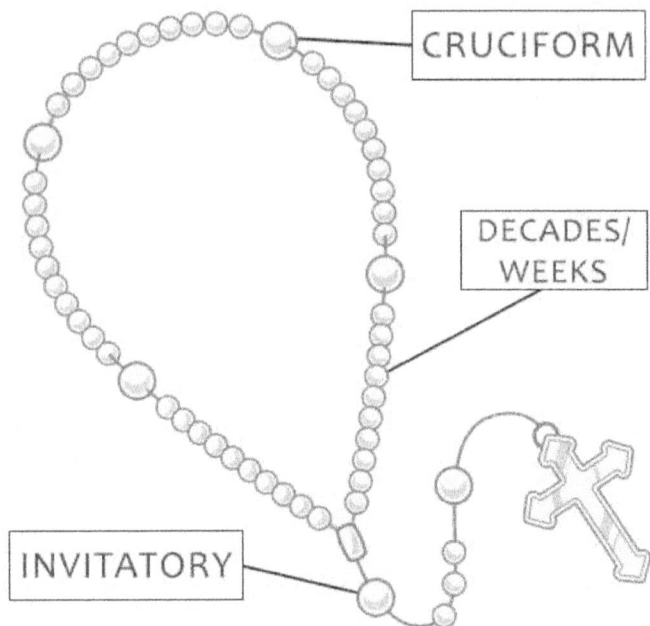

A typical Catholic Rosary, similar in style to the Anglican prayer beads.

Original design by Freepik.

* * *

How to Pray the Anglican Beads

There are a few variations to this in the next chapter which you can also follow.

1. Make the Sign of the Cross.
2. Holding the Cross, say the *Lord's Prayer.*
3. On the first bead, say the *Invitatory Prayer.*
4. On the Cruciform beads (the four slightly larger beads), say one of the relevant prayers of your choice from the previous chapter.
5. On the Weeks (the seven smaller beads between the Cruciforms), say the *Jesus Prayer*, or choose another of the relevant prayers from the previous chapter.
6. Repeat three times (as symbolism for the Trinity).
7. On the last time, say the *Lord's Prayer* on the Invitatory bead.
8. On the last time as the final prayer on the cross, say a *blessing* prayer, or a *Glory Be.*

* * *

How to Pray the Rosary

1. Make the Sign of the Cross.
2. Holding the Crucifix, say the *Apostles' Creed.*
3. On the first bead, say an *Our Father.*
4. Say one *Hail Mary* on each of the next three beads.
5. Say the *Glory Be*

6. For each of the five decades, announce the Mystery (per-haps followed by a brief reading from Scripture) then say the *Our Father*.

7. While fingering each of the ten beads of the decade, next say ten Hail Marys while meditating on the Mystery. Then say a *Glory Be*.

8. (After finishing each decade, some say the following prayer requested by the Blessed Virgin Mary at Fatima: *O my Jesus, forgive us our sins, save us from the fires of hell; lead all souls to Heaven, especially those who have most need of your mercy.*)

9. After saying the five decades, say the Hail, Holy Queen, followed by this dialogue and prayer:

10. V. Pray for us, O holy Mother of God.

11. R. That we may be made worthy of the promises of Christ.

12. *Let us pray: O God, whose Only Begotten Son, by his life, Death, and Resurrection, has purchased for us the rewards of eternal life, grant, we beseech thee, that while meditating on these mysteries of the most holy Rosary of the Blessed Virgin Mary, we may imitate what they contain and obtain what they promise, through the same Christ our Lord. Amen.*

* * *

How to Pray with an Orthodox Prayer Rope

1. Make the Sign of the Cross.
2. Begin with the *Trisagion* and *Our Father*.
3. Thumb over each knot saying *the Jesus Prayer*.

4. If there are beads present, you could use these to say *"Most Holy Theotokos save us"*, or a *Trinitarian blessing.*
5. Repeat as many times as necessary.

* * *

Icons

In Eastern Christian traditions, especially within Eastern Orthodoxy and Eastern Catholicism, holy images play a significant part in personal worship. Religious images which depict Christ, the Virgin Mary as well as the saints and angels are referred to as *icons* which serve as visual representations of God. It is important to note that these works of art are not decorations but rather they are believed by their users to be serving as divine windows thus helping them in focusing prayers and meditation. Bowing down, lighting candles and kissing is how believers venerate icons; however this does not apply because it symbolizes respect for figures depicted and not objects themselves. This connection with the sacred through icons leads worshippers into a spiritual experience where they feel united with other holy people thereby making them feel closer to God.

Traditional Icons.
Left: Christ Pantocrator; Right: The Nativity

* * *

All of these practices are ways that have been created over the centuries to try and live up to the Scriptural guidance and encouragement to "Continue steadfastly in prayer, watching in it with thanksgiving" (Colossians 4:2), and to "Pray without ceasing" (1 Thessalonians 5:17), all so that we can declare that "I will bless Yahweh at all times. His praise will always be in my mouth" (Psalm 34:1).

Recommended Retailers

If you would like to get your own icons or prayer beads/Rosary to aid in your worship, I recommend the following online shops:

Holy Art: HolyArt.com
 Holy Art is an online store that sells religious art, original sacred products and religious handmade items.
 - Use the code **SF10** for an exclusive 10% discount.

Ave Maria Every Day: avemariaeveryday.etsy.com
 Inspiring prayer in every day- anytime and anywhere

Paisley Honey Co: paisleyhoneyco.etsy.com
 Suburban bee keepers and makers of beautiful objects
 - Use the code **LectioDivina25** for an exclusive 25% discount for all prayer beads once per customer.

Celtic Orthodox Gifts: celtic-orthodox-gifts.instantecom.shop
 Handmade Chotki's, prayer ropes, icons, and prints.

12

Liturgical Prayers

The following prayers are designed to be used with prayer rope or beads (sometime called a *chaplet*) or a rosary. A chaplet is a form of prayer which uses prayer beads, and which is quite similar to but also distinct from the Rosary.

If you're unsure how to pray, liturgical prayer offers guidance, showing us the method of prayer that the Church has followed since Christ established it over 2000 years ago.

Liturgical prayer brings the Church together in a unified voice and supplication, fulfilling Jesus' command for His followers to be one.

Moreover, our prayers reflect our beliefs. Therefore, by engaging in liturgical prayer, we deepen our understanding of the faith. Contemplating the scriptures helps us focus our minds on God and allows us to become more aware of His presence in our lives.

This is sometimes summed up in the 5th century Latin phrase *lex orandi, lex credendi* meaning "the law of what is prayed [is] the law of what is believed".[2] This is sometimes expanded as *lex orandi, lex credendi, lex vivendi* meaning, "the law of what is prayed [is] what is believed [is] the law of what is lived".

In other words, *our words matter* as there is an integral link between what we pray and what we believe; the words we use to pray and worship both reveal and shape our theology.

* * *

Prayer of St. Francis Anglican Rosary

The Cross

In the name of God, Creator, Redeemer, and Sanctifier of life.

The Invitatory

O God lead us from death to life, from falsehood to truth. Lead us from despair to hope, from fear to trust. Lead us from hate to love, from war to peace. Let your peace that passes understanding fill our hearts and our world.

The Cruciforms

Lord, make me an instrument of your peace.

---

[2] The original maxim is found in the eighth book of **Prosper of Aquitaine** from the 5th Century. He was a disciple of Augustine of Hippo and wrote on the authority of the past bishops of the Apostolic See in Rome:

"Let us consider the sacraments of priestly prayers, which having been handed down by the apostles are celebrated uniformly throughout the whole world and in every Catholic Church so that the law of praying might establish the law of believing"

—Prosper of Aquitaine

The Weeks *(each phrase on a separate bead)*
Where there is hatred, let me sow love.
Where there is injury, let me sow pardon.
Where there is discord, let me sow union.
Where there is doubt, let me sow faith.
Where there is despair, let me sow hope.
Where there is darkness, let me sow light.
Where there is sadness, let me sow joy.

The Invitatory *(Last time through)*
The Lord's Prayer

The Cross
O God, grant that I may not so much seek to be consoled as to console; to be understood as to understand; to be loved as to love. For it is in giving that I receive; it is in pardoning that I am pardoned; and it is in dying that I am born to eternal life.

* * *

Anglican Chaplet

The Cross
In the Name of God, Father, Son, and Holy Spirit. *Amen.*

The Invitatory
O God make speed to save me (us),
O Lord make haste to help me (us),
Glory to the Father, and to the Son, and to the Holy Spirit:
As it was in the beginning, is now, and will be forever. *Amen.*

The Cruciforms
> Holy God,
> Holy Almighty,
> Holy Immortal One,
> Have mercy upon me (us).

The Weeks
> Lord Jesus Christ, Son of God,
> Have mercy on me, a sinner.

The Lord's Prayer (on the Invitatory bead on your last time around)
> Our Father, who art in heaven,
> hallowed be thy Name,
> thy kingdom come, thy will be done,
> on earth as it is in heaven.
> Give us this day our daily bread.
> And forgive us our trespasses,
> as we forgive those who trespass against us.
> And lead us not into temptation,
> but deliver us from evil.
> For thine is the kingdom,
> and the power, and the glory,
> forever and ever. Amen.

The Cross (on the third time around to close your chaplet)
> I bless the Lord.
> (Let us bless the Lord
> Thanks be to God.)

* * *

Trisagion and Jesus Prayer

The Cross

In the Name of God, Father, Son, and Holy Spirit. *Amen.*

The Invitatory

O God make speed to save me (us),
O Lord make haste to help me (us),
Glory to the Father, and to the Son, and to the Holy Spirit:
As it was in the beginning, is now, and will be forever. *Amen.*

The Cruciforms

Holy God,
Holy and Mighty,
Holy Immortal One,
Have mercy upon me (us)

The Weeks

Lord Jesus Christ, Son of God, Have mercy on me, a sinner.

* * *

Come Lord Jesus Prayer

The Cross

"Amen! Blessing, glory, wisdom, thanksgiving, honour, power, and might, be to our God forever and ever!
Amen." —Revelation 7:12

The Invitatory

God is our refuge and strength, a very present help in trouble.—Psalm 46:1

The Cruciforms

Praise Yahweh, my soul! All that is within me, praise his holy name!—Psalm 103:1

The Weeks

Come Lord Jesus, draw us to yourself.—John 12:32

* * *

The Hail Mary

Hail, Mary, full of grace,
   the Lord is with thee.
   Blessed art thou amongst women
   and blessed is the fruit of thy womb, Jesus.
   Holy Mary, Mother of God,
   pray for us sinners,
   now and at the hour of our death.
   Amen.

* * *

The Our Father / Lord's Prayer

Traditional

Our Father, who art in heaven,
   hallowed be thy name;
   thy kingdom come;
   thy will be done;
   on earth as it is in heaven.
   Give us this day our daily bread.
   And forgive us our trespasses,
   as we forgive those who trespass against us.
   And lead us not into temptation;
   but deliver us from evil (or *the evil one*).
   For thine is the kingdom,
   the power and the glory,
   for ever and ever.
   Amen.

Contemporary

Our Father in heaven,
   holy is your name,
   your kingdom come,
   your will be done,
   on earth as in heaven.
   Give us today our daily bread.
   Forgive us our sins
   as we forgive those who sin against us.
   Lead us not into temptation
   but deliver us from evil (or *the evil one*).
   For the kingdom, the power,
   and the glory are yours

now and for ever.
Amen.

* * *

The Doxology / Glory Be

Glory be to the Father, the Son, and the Holy Spirit. As it was in the beginning is now and ever shall be, world without end. *Amen.*

* * *

The Jesus Prayer

Lord Jesus Christ, Son of God, have mercy on me, a sinner.

* * *

Trinitarian Blessing

In the Name of God, Father, Son, and Holy Spirit. *Amen.*

* * *

Trisagion Prayers ("thrice-holy")

The Trisagion Prayers *are a set of ancient prayers that are commonly used to begin your own private prayers, often repeated three times.*

- Holy God, Holy Mighty, Holy Immortal, have mercy on us.
- Glory to Thee, our God, Glory to Thee.
- O Heavenly King, Comforter, the Spirit of Truth, Who art everywhere present and fillest all things, the Treasury of good things and Giver of life: Come, and abide in us, and cleanse us from every stain, and save our souls, O Good One.
- Holy God, Holy Mighty, Holy Immortal: have mercy on us.
- Glory to the Father, and to the Son, and to the Holy Spirit, both now and ever, and unto the ages of ages. *Amen.*
- All-Holy Trinity, have mercy on us. Lord, cleanse us from our sins. Master, pardon our iniquities. Holy God, visit and heal our infirmities for Thy name's sake.
- Lord, have mercy. Christ, have mercy. Lord, have mercy.
- Glory to the Father, and to the Son, and to the Holy Spirit, both now and ever, and unto the ages of ages.
- *Kyrie Eleison* ("Lord have Mercy")

13

The Apostles Creed

The faith of Christianity is revealed in the Holy Scriptures and set forth in the words of the Apostles' Creed, which has been recited by Christians for nearly 2000 years. It is sometimes recited as part of the *Invitatory Prayer* when praying the Rosary or similar.

* * *

I believe in God, the Father almighty,
   creator of heaven and earth.
   I believe in Jesus Christ, his only Son, our Lord,
   who was conceived by the Holy Spirit,
   born of the Virgin Mary,
   suffered under Pontius Pilate,
   was crucified, died, and was buried;
   he descended to the dead.
   On the third day he rose again;
   he ascended into heaven,
   he is seated at the right hand of the Father,

and he will come to judge the living and the dead.

I believe in the Holy Spirit,
    the holy catholic Church,
    the communion of saints,
    the forgiveness of sins,
    the resurrection of the body,
    and the life everlasting.
    Amen.

14

Selected Books

Reading Scripture with the Church Fathers
  by Christopher A Hall

Wisdom from the Ancients: 30 Forgotten Lessons from the
Early Church
  by Bryan M. Litfin

Finding Our Way Again: The Return of the Ancient Practices
(Ancient Practices Series)
  by Brian D. McLaren

The Big Book of Christian Mysticism: The Essential Guide to
Contemplative Spirituality
  by Carl Mccolman

The Essential Writings of Christian Mysticism (Modern Library
Classics)
  by Bernard McGinn

Introducing Eastern Orthodox Theology
by Andrew Louth

The Pursuit of the Holy: A Divine Invitation
by Simon Ponsonby

The Anglican Understanding of the Church: An introduction
by Paul Avis

Liturgical Year: The Spiraling Adventure of the Spiritual Life -
The Ancient Practices Series
by Joan Chittister

Common Prayer: A Liturgy for Ordinary Radicals
by Shane Claiborne, Jonathan Wilson-Hartgrove, Enuma Okoro

Getting Started with the Daily Office in the Household: A Prayer
Guide for Individuals and Families (Prayer in the Household
Series)
by The Trinity Mission, Michael Thorne Jarrett

Spirit and Sacrament: An Invitation to Eucharismatic Worship
by Andrew Wilson

Finding Sanctuary: Monastic steps for Everyday Life
by Christopher Jamison

The Chaplet of St. Francis

The Ladder of Monks
by Guigo II the Carthusian

The Healing Light Paperback
  by Agnes Sanford

The Sacred Way: Spiritual Practices for Everyday Life
  by Tony Jones

The Book of Common Prayer
  by The Church of England

About the Author

Luke holds a BA (Hons) in Biblical Studies and Theology from the University of Wales and has further specialised in areas such as *Western Christianity (200-1650)* through Yale University, *Magic in the Middle Ages* via the University of Barcelona, and *The Bible's Prehistory, Purpose, and Political Future* from Emory University. He has spent over seven years independently studying the works of the Early Church Fathers. After participating in short-term missions to South Africa, Luke co-founded WebBoss Ltd, a web development software company, with his father, Kevin. He currently resides in Devon, England.

When not working on his company or a new book, Luke writes frequently on his theological blog, *The Sacred Faith*, creates apologetic content for YouTube and TikTok, and tries to read more books than he has time for. He also enjoys spending time with his wife, Lucy, and their daughter, Amelia.

You can connect with me on:

- https://lukejwilson.com
- https://x.com/mrlewk
- https://www.facebook.com/LukeJWilsonAuthor
- https://thesacredfaith.co.uk
- https://www.patreon.com/LukeJWilson
- https://tiktok.com/@lukejwilsonauthor

Subscribe to my newsletter:

- https://lukejwilson.com/cmd/subscribe.html

Also by Luke J. Wilson

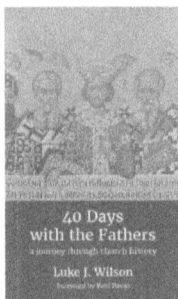

40 DAYS WITH THE FATHERS: A Journey Through Church History
Take a journey through the first 400 years of Church History in only 40 days!

Over the course of this reading plan you will read extracts and commentary on 23 different early Church texts from a selection of some of the most influential Church Fathers:

Didache, Diognetus, Polycarp, Ignatius, Justin Martyr, Cyprian, Athanasius, Cyril of Jerusalem, Ambrose of Milan, and Leo the Great.

These people who came before us, those great men of faith, many of whom suffered persecution and martyrdom to preserve the Church and Christ's mission, bridge the gap between the Bible and the present day. They fill the void we sometimes wonder about when we get to the end of reading Acts or the Epistles and think, *"what happened next?"* or *"what happened to the Ephesian church after Paul left?"* — well now you can read for yourself and see how God continued to grow His Church!

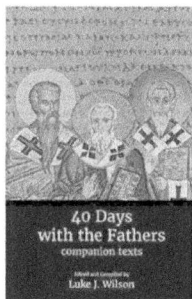

40 DAYS WITH THE FATHERS: Companion Texts

This book is the companion to 40 Days with the Fathers: A Daily Reading Plan, and includes twenty-three Early Church texts in full—including all additional footnotes from the original editors and translators so that you can get as close as possible to reading these ancient texts without needing to know ancient Greek or Latin.

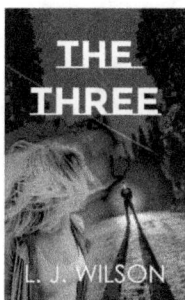

The Three

Mystery, intrigue and secrets.

Katie Jones just wanted to start her life after college, but one rainy day changed everything, forever... Moving to a sleepy village in Cornwall was meant to be a nice new start for Katie. That was until a rainy day changed everything in a single moment, making her life change in ways she could never have anticipated. Now with secrets about the world around her being revealed, strange men appearing from the shadows telling her mystical things, and a whole new world of possibilities opening up - how will Katie cope with all the new information? But it's not all exciting; now she must learn to fight for survival to escape with her life still intact! Life would never be the same again.

www.ingramcontent.com/pod-product-compliance
Lightning Source LLC
LaVergne TN
LVHW051409080426
835508LV00022B/2999